Praise for *T*

Nate Pickowicz's wonderful vo[...]
ment for weary souls. He has ta[...] [...] goodness of
God as reflected in His manifold kindnesses to undeserving sinners
in the same spirit as the Puritans of yesteryear: deeply pastoral, rich
in Scripture, and profound in application. If you are struggling with
how good God truly is while living in a cruel world or simply need to
be reminded of the broad expressions of His lovingkindness in every
area of your life, then this book is for you! Devour its contents and
find nourishment for your starving soul.

SCOTT CHRISTENSEN
Associate Pastor, Kerrville Bible Church, Kerrville, TX; author
of *What about Free Will?* and *What about Evil?*

A sweet encouragement for weary souls! In a world filled with so
much suffering and cruelty, the message of *The Kindness of God* comes
as a welcome balm. God is not withholding or reluctant in His goodness toward His people; He is kind. Pickowicz helps readers grasp just
how thoroughly the theme of God's kindness penetrates the Scriptures and overflows to every area of our lives. Highly recommended!

REAGAN ROSE
Founder of Redeeming Productivity

In a world that equates kindness with mere niceness, this book is
a biblical corrective. Pickowicz shows from Scripture that God's
kindness is a merciful expression of His goodness—that is, the
unchanging standard of what is right and pure. In *The Kindness of
God*, we are reminded that our Father loves to give good gifts to His
children—especially the gift of His lovingkindness toward us in every
circumstance and season of our lives.

ABIGAIL DODDS
Author of *Bread of Life*, *(A) Typical Woman*, and *A Student's Guide to
Womanhood*

The Kindness of God is a refreshing cup of cold water in the shallow, arid climate of twenty-first-century American Christianity. This is a book of rich theology, overflowing with Scripture, that reads like a novel. It is deep yet engaging, simple yet smart, strong yet encouraging, insightful yet practical. Following along with Pastor Nate as he explores the theme of God's kindness throughout the Bible will do your soul well, as it has mine!

JON BENZINGER
Lead Pastor of Redeemer Bible Church, Gilbert, AZ; author of *Stand: Christianity vs. Social Justice*

As I read this book by my friend, Nate Pickowicz, I was greatly encouraged and refreshed in my own soul by the truth that God's kindness toward me in Christ is unending. As *The Kindness of God* shows, God's kindness toward His children is one of those truths that ravishes the Christian mind. It leaves us spellbound by the sweetness of His mercy and grace toward undeserving sinners. Pastorally speaking, I think it is one of the great truths of which we need to be reminded of again and again. So I am thankful for this book, and I hope it gains a wide reading. Its message is desperately needed.

GRANT CASTLEBERRY
Senior Pastor of Capital Community Church, Raleigh, NC; president and Bible teacher of Unashamed Truth Ministries

THE KINDNESS OF GOD

*Beholding His Goodness
in a Cruel World*

NATE PICKOWICZ

MOODY PUBLISHERS

CHICAGO

Edited by Philip F. Newman
Interior design: Kaylee Dunn, Puckett Smartt
Cover design: Erik M. Peterson
Cover photo of ruins copyright © 2023 by liuzishan/Adobe Stock (360866146).
Cover graphic of watercolor background copyright © 2023 by Kwang Gallery/Adobe Stock (484812189).
Cover graphic of light beams copyright © 2023 by kokotewan/Adobe Stock (374905691).
All rights reserved for all of the images above.
Author photo: Carla Howe

Library of Congress Cataloging-in-Publication Data

Names: Pickowicz, Nathan, author.
Title: The kindness of God : beholding his goodness in a cruel world /
    Nathan Pickowicz.
Description: Chicago : Moody Publishers, [2024] | Includes bibliographical
    references. | Summary: "Kindness has fallen on hard times. Pastor and
    author Nate Pickowicz shows how our lives must be understood and lived
    in the knowledge of God's kindness. This book offers biblical salve to
    weary souls. In a world that can feel dark and cold, discover the light
    of God's kindness!"-- Provided by publisher.
Identifiers: LCCN 2023032405 (print) | LCCN 2023032406 (ebook) | ISBN
    9780802431806 | ISBN 9780802472892 (ebook)
Subjects: LCSH: Kindness--Religious aspects--Christianity. |
    Kindness--Biblical teaching.
Classification: LCC BJ1533.K5 P54 2024 (print) | LCC BJ1533.K5 (ebook) |
    DDC 177/.7--dc23/eng/20230926
LC record available at https://lccn.loc.gov/2023032405
LC ebook record available at https://lccn.loc.gov/2023032406

Originally delivered by fleets of horse-drawn wagons, the affordable paperbacks from D. L. Moody's publishing house resourced the church and served everyday people. Now, after more than 125 years of publishing and ministry, Moody Publishers' mission remains the same—even if our delivery systems have changed a bit. For more information on other books (and resources) created from a biblical perspective, go to www.moodypublishers.com or write to:

Moody Publishers
820 N. LaSalle Boulevard
Chicago, IL 60610

1 3 5 7 9 10 8 6 4 2

Printed in the United States of America

To my mom

CONTENTS

BEHOLDING THE KINDNESS OF GOD

---

*The LORD is righteous in all His ways
and kind in all His deeds.* (**Ps.** 145:17)

Susan had a hard life. After being diagnosed with Crohn's disease at fourteen years old, she would endure a lifetime of compounding sicknesses. Always plagued with varying levels of pain and discomfort, she eventually developed glaucoma, rheumatoid arthritis, and severe kidney stones, which required extensive and invasive treatments. Surgery was part of her life at many times, and pain was a constant unwanted companion.

Growing up, Susan had been abused by her brothers, classmates, and even her father, who on one occasion knocked out several of her teeth. She had a baby girl at age eighteen but sadly had to give her up for adoption due to her inability to care for her in the midst of sickness and hospitalizations. Marriage to her first husband brought two more children, but also more abuse. She would remarry again, but after only three years, he packed up and left her with nothing but a small disability income and no options. Unable to afford her home, she ended up moving to a run-down apartment with a ceiling that was caving in.

And then one day she found a lump.

Susan's breast cancer was only exacerbated by her Crohn's disease, which also made radiation and chemotherapy a torturous experience. Before long, she endured a double mastectomy to remove the cancer. Within a year, however, it had returned and metastasized to her brain. Despite an eight-hour brain surgery, the cancer still progressed.

While still living in her dilapidated apartment, her condition began to worsen, and she began falling. Her family searched for a treatment facility that would take her in, but the local hospice had no available beds. And so, her mother and daughter attempted to create a makeshift hospital room at home, staffed by various friends and women from her mother's church who would come and sit up with her through the agonizing nights. Finally, when a bed opened up in a hospice facility forty-five minutes away, she was moved. It would be her last home.

Throughout her life, no matter the circumstances, Susan always tried to stay positive. Yet trouble always seemed to stalk her. Despite all her attempts to be happy, the cancer proved too great an enemy. As her illness progressed, her mind and her body began to break down. She experienced terrifying hallucinations and delirium, as is common with brain cancer patients. After a painful, grueling battle, Susan finally passed away at age fifty-four.

When we hear about stories like Susan's, it's natural to ask, "How could a good God allow for such a terrible thing? Why would a kind, loving God afflict a woman with such a difficult life that came to an end through a horrendous disease?" Skeptics and critics will conclude that God is either powerless or cruel—but certainly not *kind*. They would claim that a world full of pain and suffering is undoubtedly the proof of it. However, this challenge needs to be met with some hard truth.

THE CRUELTY OF EVIL IN THE FACE OF GOD'S GOODNESS

Our news feeds are cluttered with stories of terrible events. I remember reading about a young mother who went out jogging only to be abducted by two men and taken back to their house where she was sexually and violently assaulted, tortured, and starved within an inch of her life. After several weeks of unthinkable hell, she was dumped off on the side of the road, naked and emaciated, where she died alone.

But even our more common, everyday experiences bear witness to the cruelty of this world. A father who abandons his family to ruin in order to pursue another life. A teenager who overdoses on methamphetamines. A child who commits suicide after being tormented by peers at school. An illness that forces a family into bankruptcy and homelessness.

THE KINDNESS OF GOD

An elderly woman who is abused in a nursing home as she slowly and painfully declines from the debilitating effects of Alzheimer's disease.

When we encounter awful situations like these and hear the refrain, "How could a good God allow such things?" we need to check ourselves and examine our own judgment. Attacking the character of God over the wickedness committed by human beings overlooks the depravity of the human heart. The real question that should be asked is, "How could anyone commit such an evil act against another human being?" This leads us into addressing the problem of sin.

The Bible records the events that took place "in the beginning" (Gen. 1:1). God created all things—the heavens and the earth, the moon and the stars, the sea and the land, plants and animals, and finally, human beings. He created everything to be "very good" (Gen. 1:31). Everything was as it should be. But then Adam and Eve disobeyed God by violating His command not to eat of the tree that was forbidden to them. However, the transgression was not about eating the wrong kind of fruit, but about willful rebellion against the Creator.

When the first humans rebelled against God, they fell from their good standing with Him, and evil entered the world. In fact, the Bible teaches us that it was "through one man [that] sin entered into the world, and death through sin" (Rom. 5:12). With the entrance of sin and death into the world, the whole created order became enslaved to corruption and began to "groan and suffer the pains of

childbirth" (Rom. 8:21–22). In short, the fall of humanity
plunged everything into chaos and destruction. To illustrate
just how wicked things became, we should remember that
the third person ever to exist killed the fourth (Gen. 4:8).[1]

All these millennia later, the world is still drowning in a
sea of sin and wickedness. It permeates all aspects of life, and
nothing escapes its deadly grasp. Plants shrivel and die; animals savagely attack each other; children get cancer; mobs
brutally murder innocent bystanders; crooked businessmen
steal millions from destitute people; tidal waves wipe out
unsuspecting villages—all as a result of the curse of the fall.

And yet, we may be tempted to blame God for the evil we
see in the world. But the Bible teaches that God is not the
author of sin and evil (e.g., Ps. 5:4).[2] Furthermore, He does
not tempt anyone to commit sin (James 1:13). Rather, God
is good, and all His ways are right and true (Deut. 32:4; Ps.
33:4; cf. 1 John 1:5). The reason a woman dies of breast cancer
is not due to any deficiency in the character of God, but rather
it is a result of the widespread effects of humanity's fall into sin
and wickedness. But God is still good; He is still kind.

While we are in the world, however, we experience the
devastating effects of sin's curse. Terrible things happen.
People hurt us. We hurt others. All told, it's hard to escape
the reality that we are living in an increasingly cruel world.
But where do we look for hope? Where do we find goodness,
kindness, and love? As we will see, the only oasis of goodness
is found in God.

GOODNESS AND KINDNESS

When Moses marched up Mount Sinai to meet with God, his burning curiosity led him to ask, "I pray You, show me Your glory!" (Ex. 33:18). Not without some conditions, the Lord granted the request and proclaimed, "I Myself will make all My goodness pass before you" (v. 19). In the next chapter, we find ourselves hidden with Moses in the cleft of the rock, beholding God's back as He passes by, declaring,

> *The LORD, the LORD God,* compassionate and gracious, *slow to anger, and* abounding in lovingkindness *and truth; who keeps lovingkindness for thousands, who forgives iniquity, transgression and sin; yet He will by no means leave the guilty unpunished, visiting the iniquity of fathers on the children and on the grandchildren to the third and fourth generations. (Ex. 34:6–7, emphasis added)*

In this astounding display, God not only flashes forth His visible glory, but also declares various truths about Himself—*perfections*, or *attributes*, as they're called by theologians. God expresses to Moses the aspects of who He is. And while the list is not completely exhaustive, we learn of His compassion, grace, patience, lovingkindness, truthfulness, forgiveness, and justice. However, the Lord Himself refers to all of what He reveals to Moses as His *goodness*.

God's goodness is the ultimate standard of all that is morally pure, inherently right, and worthy of approval. Any judgment of something being good has to be stacked up against God Himself, for He is the barometer of all goodness. Furthermore, God's goodness encompasses all of His divine perfections, as all of them display God's intrinsic goodness. Stephen Charnock notes, "All good meets in his essence, as all water meets in the ocean."[3]

When we look in the Bible, we see that the Hebrew word *tûb* can refer to goodness, good things, prosperity, fairness, or even beauty. But when describing God, it refers to His perfect and upright character. The psalmist confesses, "How great is Your *goodness*, which You have stored up for those who fear You, which You have wrought for those who take refuge in You, before the sons of men!" (Ps. 31:19, emphasis added). Isaiah extolled the character of God when he declared, "I shall make mention of the lovingkindnesses of the LORD, the praises of the LORD, according to all that the LORD has granted us, and the great *goodness* toward the house of Israel, which He has granted them according to His compassion and according to the abundance of His lovingkindnesses" (Isa. 63:7, emphasis added). Speaking of the future restoration of Israel, we read, "'I will fill the soul of the priests with abundance, and My people will be satisfied with My *goodness*,' declares the LORD" (Jer. 31:14, emphasis added). Repeatedly we behold the objective goodness of God displayed before His people.

However, the goodness of God functions almost as an umbrella that encompasses many other of His divine perfections. William G. T. Shedd refers to God's goodness as "a special attribute with varieties under it."[4] One of the key "varieties" of God's goodness is His *kindness*. Louis Berkhof notes, "The goodness of God should not be confused with His kindness, which is a more restricted concept." They are not the same thing. However, he continues, "in our ascription of goodness to God the fundamental idea is that He is in every way all that He as God should be, and therefore answers perfectly to the ideal expressed in the word 'God.' He is good in the metaphysical sense of the word, absolute perfection and perfect bliss in Himself."[5]

Or to further distinguish, Wilhelmus à Brakel notes, "From this goodness issues forth lovingkindness and an inclination to bless His creatures."[6] To help distinguish between *goodness* and *kindness*, we ought to note that God's goodness is His intrinsic character, while His kindness is the outward expression of it toward His people. It is *out of* God's goodness that we experience His kindness.

In the Bible, this kindness is expressed in several different words. The Hebrew word *hesed*, which is often translated as "lovingkindness," appears nearly 250 times in the Old Testament, while Greek words like *chrēstotēs* (e.g., 2 Cor. 9:6; Gal. 5:22), *agathos* (e.g., Acts 9:36), *eudokia* (e.g., Eph. 1:5, 9), and *epieikeia* (e.g., Acts 24:4) have been variously rendered "kindness" in some English translations. Of course, these words are used in many different contexts and should not all be translated "kindness" in every case. However, for our purposes, we will define God's kindness as *the demonstration of His goodness toward His people*.

KEEPING IT SIMPLE

The task of studying and understanding truths about God feels like trying to wrap your arms around the Rock of Gibraltar. It's just too big, too wide, and too heavy! However, we are encouraged to know God (John 17:3) and seek to understand Him (Col. 1:9–10). But in exploring God's goodness and kindness, we need to make a few clarifications.

Christians have always believed that God is triune—one God who exists eternally in three distinct persons: the Father, the Son, and the Holy Spirit. Because each member of the Trinity is God, each divine person fully and truly possesses the same divine perfections. As the ancient Athanasian Creed declares, "We worship one God in Trinity, and Trinity in Unity." No member of the Trinity is more God than another; each person is God. The creed continues, "The Godhead of the Father, of the Son, and of the Holy Spirit is all one, the glory equal, the majesty coeternal."[7] And so, what is true of the Father is also true of the Son, as well as the Holy Spirit. However, the primary focus of this book will be on the Father, in what we call *theology proper*—the character and attributes of God in general. However, as examples arise, we will also discuss how the kindness of God is expressed in the Son and in the Holy Spirit.

The second clarification pertains to how we actually understand the being of God. Through the course of church history, theologians have given us various terms to explain complicated concepts. When apprehending God, we understand that He is *simple*. This is not to say that He is in any way simplistic, as though you could add up all of His attributes and arrive at "God," but rather that He is pure God—a God without parts. This is what is known as the doctrine of *divine simplicity*. In other words, God is one (Deut. 6:4), and not the sum of all His divine attributes. He is not *part* love, *part* justice, *part* goodness, *part* omnipotence, *part* grace, *part* mercy, and so on. Rather, God is *all* love. He is *all* justice. He is *all* graciousness. He is *all* mercy. He is *all* kindness. Said another way, all that is in God is purely and truly God.[8]

If we were to attempt an analogy, we might say that we behold God as light through a diamond. Each new look reveals the same light refracted through the many sides of the same beautiful gemstone, yet the many-splendored colors and shapes appear unique to us. As we focus our study on one particular attribute of God—His *kindness*—our aim is to turn the diamond so that only one spectrum of color shines forth. As we explore this one attribute, it is not to the neglect of the others, but rather for the purpose of focusing in on a few of the ways God's goodness is specifically expressed to us in His lovingkindness.

THE GRAND PREMISE

As we examine the aspects of God's kindness displayed in various situations, I believe it will help us to work from a single basic premise. In order to give us some framework with which to understand God's kindness to us, I want to offer a working thesis. I'm calling it "the Grand Premise." It is as follows:

> *God is good; we are sinful. Because of this, we are undeserving of His goodness. But because of God's mercy, He demonstrates lovingkindness to us. Therefore, every kindness we experience is pure grace and ought to be received with gladness and thankfulness.*

We will examine this Grand Premise in greater depth throughout the book, as it will serve as the backdrop to understanding every component of God's kindness to us. However, let us take a brief look at the premise here.

First, *God is good.* We have already touched on this earlier and will explore His goodness in subsequent chapters, but God's goodness is the basis of our Grand Premise. It is imperative that we reconcile in our minds that God's character, nature, judgments, and actions are totally and completely good. He can do no wrong; there is no evil within Him.

Second, *we are sinful.* Adam and Eve's rebellion in the garden of Eden plunged the human race into condemnation and death because of sinfulness. This is what is known as the fall, which places us on the receiving end of God's righteous judgment. We will cover this more in the next chapter.

Third, *Because of this, we are undeserving of God's goodness.* Our sinful rebellion against God renders us as enemies and undeserving of anything good that God could give us (1 Chron. 17:16; Rom. 4:2–5). Whatever we receive from the Lord is pure grace.

Fourth, *Because of God's mercy, He demonstrates loving-kindness to us.* At this point, we appeal to God's own character, namely His mercy toward undeserving people. God's mercy is not based on the worthiness of the person receiving it, but on His own lovingkindness. We will see this expressed through many circumstances in chapters 1 through 6.

Finally, we arrive at the conclusion: *Therefore every kindness we experience is pure grace and ought to be received with gladness and thankfulness.* This is our response to God's kindness, which we will explore in chapter 7, as well as the required response from the nations under the sovereign hand of God in chapter 8.

BETTER THAN LIFE

Psalm 63 was written by David at a time when he was in great emotional distress. Driven away from his home in Jerusalem and into the wilderness, he was (many Bible scholars believe) likely fleeing from his son Absalom who was trying to kill him and supplant him as king (2 Sam. 15:13–37). However, despite being driven into the desert wilderness, David had also been driven into a greater desert—the desert of his own desperation.

In great despair and anguish, David turns to the Lord and professes, "Oh God, You are my God; I shall seek You earnestly; my soul thirsts for You, my flesh yearns for You, in a dry and weary land where there is no water" (v. 1). In the midst of great distress, David cries out for God, longing to return to Jerusalem where he can worship the Lord in His temple. His desire is to behold the majesty of the Lord: "Thus I have seen You in the sanctuary, to see Your power and Your glory" (v. 2). Despite the cruelty David has experienced from others—even his own son!—he longs for the restorative presence of God.

But then David remembers and rehearses the goodness of God to him. "Because *Your lovingkindness is better than life*, my lips will praise You" (v. 3, emphasis added). Keep in mind that David is teetering on the brink of death, yet He confesses that the lovingkindness of the Lord is *better than life*! Better than safety and security; better than power and prosperity; better than the praises of men and the adoration of family; better than health and wellness; better even than all that a king could obtain—God's kindness is supreme.

Because of this, David declares, "So I will bless You as long as I live; I will lift up my hands in Your name. My soul is satisfied as with marrow and fatness, and my mouth offers praises with joyful lips" (vv. 4–5). David is determined to remember and extol the kindness of God no matter what happens in his life. However, is this our own perspective? When we look at the world around us, or the difficult situations in our own life, do we regard God's kindnesses to us as better than anything else? Better even than life?! Our challenge is to see our own life in this light.

The aim of this book is twofold. We will explore the character of God, especially His divine goodness, out of which flows His lovingkindness. Beyond this, however, we will see examples of the kindness of God in light of all circumstances. And while, frankly, a study like this could be inexhaustible, we will look at a few key areas of life in which we can see the kindness of God displayed—namely, in salvation, repentance, sanctification, blessing, relationships, and suffering. The final two chapters will explore the kindness of God reflected in the Christian believer, followed by God's kindness to the nations. In the end, we want to be able to behold God's kindness, seeing it as *better* than all that life has to offer. And we want to rejoice with the psalmist in declaring with confidence, "The LORD is righteous in all His ways and kind in all His deeds" (Ps. 145:17).

Chapter One

GOD'S KINDNESS IN SALVATION

But when the kindness of God our Savior . . . appeared,
He saved us. (Titus 3:4–5)

They didn't deserve to be saved, at least that's how Jonah
had it worked out in his heart. The people of Nineveh
were Assyrians—mortal enemies of Israel. In fact, God's
people had suffered greatly at the hands of the Assyrians who
were often cruel to their enemies (2 Kings 19:17). Furthermore, they were an idolatrous people, worshiping false gods.
By all standards, the Assyrian Ninevites deserved God's
fierce judgment.

However, the Lord sent word to the prophet Jonah,
son of Amittai, that he was to, "Arise, go to Nineveh the
great city and cry against it, for their wickedness has come
up before Me" (Jonah 1:2). God intends to send Jonah to
preach repentance to this wicked people that they might
turn from their sinfulness and be saved (3:8). Jonah, on the
other hand, wants nothing to do with the restoration of

Israel's enemy and flees as far away as he can travel. The Lord famously pursues Jonah, sending a storm and a great fish, until finally Jonah relents and vows to obey the Lord.

In Jonah 3, he preaches against the Ninevites' wickedness, and they turn away from their sins. We read, "When God saw their deeds, that they turned from their wicked way, then God relented concerning the calamity which He had declared He would bring upon them" (v. 10). But this does not sit well with Jonah at all. He becomes angry with the Lord, not because Jonah was a malicious person, but because He could not fathom the fact that God is "a gracious and compassionate God, slow to anger and abundant in lovingkindness, and one who relents concerning calamity" (4:2); Jonah cannot tolerate God's kindness toward his enemies.

In the wake of Jonah's unrighteous anger, the Lord disciplines the weary prophet through a series of small trials (4:4–8). In the end, the Lord concludes that even if Jonah were able to have compassion on a tiny plant that provided shade over his head, then God was righteous to have compassion on the people of Nineveh. The final verse of Jonah's prophecy records the compassion of God on "more than 120,000 persons who do not know the difference between their right and left hand" (v. 11)—most likely a reference to children. With a population of likely several hundred thousand people, the salvation of Nineveh demonstrates one of the greatest single acts of divine kindness recorded in Scripture.

GOD'S SAVING KINDNESS AND THE PROBLEM OF SIN

Many people today would not think to regard the notion of *salvation* as being a particular kindness of God. Why is salvation even necessary? From what are we being saved? The reason why God's saving action is not highly valued is because of a misunderstanding of the need for salvation at all. As we briefly discussed in the introduction, the entrance of sin into the world creates a dire need for salvation. But let's look at this again.

The word *sin* is an archery term meaning "a failure to hit the mark"—to "sin" the target is to miss the bullseye. However, we understand it to be a religious word, reflecting moral or ethical failing. These days, though, we often treat sin as if it were some innocuous scuff in the cosmic continuum. We tend not to regard sin as a very serious thing. We misunderstand its significance and underestimate its power. In doing so, not only have we missed the target, but we fail to realize that it is God's standard (His bullseye) that we have missed. But what is God's standard?

In short, God's standard is perfection. When giving the people of Israel His commands, God told them "I am the LORD your God. Consecrate yourselves therefore and be holy, for I am holy" (Lev. 11:44; 20:26; cf. 1 Peter 1:16). When the Lord Jesus gave His Sermon on the Mount, He exhorted His followers once more, "Therefore you are to be perfect, as your heavenly Father is perfect" (Matt. 5:48). God demands perfection. Why does God demand perfection? Because He Himself is perfect in every way.

The Bible teaches us much about the character and attributes of God. He is all-powerful (Gen. 18:14; Matt. 19:26), ever-present (Ps. 139:7–10; Jer. 23:23–24), all-knowing (Ps. 139:3–4; Job 37:16), unchanging (Ps. 102:25–27; Mal. 3:6), transcendent (Eph. 4:6), sovereign (Rev. 1:8), truthful (Titus 1:2; Heb. 6:18), etc. However, in order to better understand why sin is such an affront to God, we need to apprehend the concept of God's *holiness* (Ps. 99:9; Isa. 1:4; 6:3). R. C. Sproul notes,

> *The Bible never says that God is love, love, love; or mercy, mercy, mercy; or wrath, wrath, wrath; or justice, justice, justice. It does say that He is holy, holy, holy, that the whole earth is full of His glory.*[1]

In Scripture, the threefold repetition "holy, holy, holy" establishes the gravity and prominence of the statement. The word *holy* means "to set apart," but with regard to God, it describes the height and depth of His perfection. In all ways, He is pure, righteous, and good. By comparison, in our attempt to be righteous, we jump like grasshoppers merely inches off the ground; God's holiness reaches the sun—93 million miles away.

In the garden of Eden, God gave Adam a command not to eat from the tree of the knowledge of good and evil, and if he disobeyed, the punishment would be death (Gen. 2:17). But by chapter 3, Eve is deceived into believing the lie that eating from the forbidden tree would make them like God Himself (v. 5). Not only did they fail to trust and obey God;

their rebellion demonstrated a rejection of God's righteous standard.

Surely God cannot tolerate spiritual insurrection, can He? Can He simply look the other way, pretending that this was only a little gaffe? Of course not! His perfect character will not allow it. His righteousness will not permit it. His sense of justice cannot comprehend it. Why? Because if God were to fail to oppose and punish sin, He would be guilty of aiding and abetting sin, which would impugn His righteous character. But that's simply not possible. Even the apostle Paul exclaimed, "May it never be!" (Rom. 6:2).

Consider a man who drinks himself into oblivion and then gets behind the wheel of his truck. On his way home from the bar, he runs a red light and kills a seventeen-year-old girl on her way back from her summertime job. When the man is brought into court for his crime, would a good judge let him go scot-free? But the man is a nice guy who does volunteer work in his community. Why not let him off with a reprimand? We understand that a good judge would not allow the man's crime to go unpunished because it would be completely unjust. Beyond the fact that the college-bound teenage girl will never live to realize her dreams, the family, who will grieve her loss for the rest of their lives, would be dishonored and sinned against if their daughter's killer walked without punishment.

And so, just as a good judge would not let this driver off, a good and holy God can't excuse our sin. In fact, what we might perceive to be even a minor sin is actually an attack on the righteous character of God. Therefore, the Bible teaches us that, apart from the saving work of Christ, God punishes even the smallest infraction with severe and righteous judgment—an eternity in hell. James 2:10 says, "For whoever keeps the whole law and yet stumbles in one point, he has become guilty of all." The Bible teaches that "the wages of sin is death" (Rom. 6:23), and further, that "all have sinned" (Rom. 3:23); none are truly righteous.

Once again, if the center bullseye is God's perfect holiness, then to *sin* the target is to fail to achieve His righteous standard. It is, in essence, to "fall short of the glory of God" (Rom. 3:23). But more than simply failing to hit a mark, the apostle John tells us that "sin is lawlessness" (1 John 3:4). Further, J. C. Ryle defines sin as "doing, saying, thinking, or imagining, anything that is not in perfect conformity with the mind and law of God."[2] It is spiritual anarchy and rebellion. More than being simply a series of flaws, missteps, peccadillos, or blunders, sin is a serious affront to the goodness and holiness of God. It is an attack on the throne of the King.

Sin is terminal, spiritual cancer—it hardens us, defiles us, degrades us, poisons us, enslaves us, kills us. But the greater impact falls not to us, but to God. Sin enrages Him, insults Him, assaults Him, undermines Him, attacks Him. And He responds with fierce wrath, burning anger, severe judgment, and eternal condemnation. To God, sin is not a light thing; it is an immense evil that is destined to be judged and eradicated.

Does this seem too harsh? If so, it is because we tend to

think of justice from a human perspective. But in truth, all sin affects someone somehow. And if we can comprehend the concept of justice in a *human* court, how much higher the demand for absolute justice must exist in the court of heaven presided over by a perfectly righteous God? In short, God *must* punish any and all sin to the fullest measure. Otherwise, He would not be truly just or righteous. Yet, in God's own kindness, He provides a way of escape for those who have broken His law.

THE LOVINGKINDNESS OF GOD

In the Old Testament, we see the salvation of God's people bound up in His own kindness toward them. The Hebrew word *hesed* (pronounced "khesed") is often translated as "lovingkindness" in many English translations. But it is also rendered in other ways, like "steadfast love" (ESV) or "covenant faithfulness," for example.[3] The key idea is that, because of God's own gracious character, He makes an unbreakable promise (covenant) to save His people. We see this expressed in Moses' song of deliverance for the Israelites: "In Your lovingkindness [*hesed*] You have led the people whom You have redeemed; in Your strength You have guided them to Your holy habitation" (Ex. 15:13, emphasis added). God does not save and redeem because it is owed to them. Rather, He saves because of His own goodness and lovingkindness.

This specific kindness of God in salvation is further demonstrated over and against the wickedness of humanity.

We read in Psalm 5,

> For You are not a God who takes pleasure in
>   wickedness;
> No evil dwells with You.
> The boastful shall not stand before Your eyes;
> You hate all who do iniquity.
> You destroy those who speak falsehood;
> The LORD abhors the man of bloodshed and
>   deceit.
> (vv. 4-6)

However, David rejoices, "But as for me, *by Your abundant lovingkindness* [*hesed*] I will enter Your house, at Your holy temple I will bow in reverence for You" (v. 7, emphasis added). Again, David is not claiming that He is granted access to God because he is somehow better than other sinners, but because of God's own "abundant lovingkindness" to him as an object of grace and mercy.

This stark contrast between human sinfulness and God's saving kindness is beautifully expressed through the marriage of Hosea. The book of Hosea tells the story of a prophet named Hosea and his wife, Gomer. In the opening chapter, we learn that Gomer has violated her marriage covenant and committed adultery. However, because of his love for his wife, Hosea forgives her and takes her back. God uses the whole ordeal as a picture of Israel's spiritual adultery against God and His own desire to restore her and receive her back to Himself. In redeeming her, the Lord declares, "I will betroth you to Me forever; yes, I will betroth you to Me in righteousness and in justice, in lovingkindness [*hesed*] and in compassion, and I will betroth you to Me in faithfulness. Then you will know the LORD" (Hos. 2:19–20). The Lord saves Israel, not because she is faithful or virtuous—she has sinned grievously!—but because God desires to save her by His own lovingkindness and steadfast love.

After Lot had embedded himself within the wicked culture of the people of Sodom, the Lord sent two angels to rescue him and his family from destruction. God, in His own righteous judgment, had every right to destroy the entire city and all its inhabitants, but He made a way for Lot's family to escape by the help of two angels. As he is fleeing the city, Lot cries out to the Lord's angels, "Now behold, your servant has found favor in your sight, and you have magnified your lovingkindness, which you have shown me by saving my life" (Gen. 19:19).

Over and over again, the lovingkindness of the Lord is extolled as the reason why He provides salvation for His people. Not that sinners deserve to be saved, but God extends His own heart to them and sets His love upon them. This remarkable act is what motivates God's people to say, "Because Your lovingkindness is better than life, my lips will praise You" (Ps. 63:3).

DYING FOR HIS ENEMIES

In many ways, the stark contrast between humanity's sinfulness and God's kindness is even more pronounced in the New Testament. While it does not include the specific language of "kindness," Romans 5 illustrates the amazing love of God to extend salvation to those who are worthy of death. In explaining the gospel to his audience, the apostle Paul reasons that, in terms of self-sacrifice, "one will hardly die for a righteous man; though perhaps for the good man someone would dare even to die" (Rom. 5:7). In other words, if our best friend was standing in oncoming traffic, it is likely that we would risk our own life to save them. Most people could conceive of dying for a righteous person.

However, Paul turns the whole thing on its head by saying, "But God demonstrates His own love toward us, in that while we were yet sinners, Christ died for us" (v. 8). And not just "sinners"—we read in verse 10 that we were even "enemies" of God! Now the illustration has changed. It's no longer the idea of someone stepping out into oncoming traffic to save their best friend; instead, the person who is about to be killed is someone who betrayed, slandered, and hurt you severely—an *enemy*! How many people would give their own life to save their sworn enemy? Nobody would do that.

Yet God essentially does something like this. In our fallen condition, we were God's own enemies. In our sinfulness, we despised God and purposed in our hearts to rebel against Him at every turn. We hated Him. This is why Ephesians 2:1–2 tells us that we "were dead in [our] trespasses and sins, in which [we] formerly walked according to the course of this world, according to the prince of the power of the air, of the spirit that is now working in the sons of disobedience."

This spiritual deadness rendered us as "children of wrath" (v. 3). Were God not to intervene on our behalf, we would be cast into the fires of judgment along with every other sinner who has ever existed.

"But God," Paul wrote, "demonstrates His own love toward us, in that while we were yet sinners"—even *enemies*—"Christ died for us." Why would God do this? It is because of His goodness and lovingkindness toward us. But how is salvation accomplished and made possible to us?

I remember when I was a kid, there was a local store owner with a bad reputation in town. He was proud, opinionated, even belligerent at times. His store was always fully stocked with large amounts of beer, cigarettes, and pornography, and he liked it that way. When Christians in town stopped by to share the gospel, he cursed at them and kicked them out of his store. But then, one day, after hearing the gospel again, he believed.

Suddenly, his whole life began to change. He started reading his Bible and praying. He began attending church, to the amazement and joy of the people in town who had been witnessing to him for years. Before long, his conscience became pricked to the point where he no longer wanted to profit off of the things that damaged other people, so he sold his store. As his love and zeal for the Lord continued to increase, his desire to share the gospel became insatiable. Today, he travels the country full-time as an evangelist. Formerly an enemy of God, he is now His servant and friend.

OUR SALVATION THROUGH CHRIST

Just like the Old Testament, the New Testament teaches that this wonderful salvation is extended to us as a *kindness*. Paul opens his letter to the Ephesians by talking about God's gracious work of salvation toward His people. In saving His people, God "chose us in Him before the foundation of the world, that we would be holy and blameless before Him. In love He predestined us to adoption as sons through Jesus Christ to Himself" (Eph. 1:4–5a). What is the basis of God's saving work? We read that it is "according to the *kind intention* of His will" (Eph. 1:5; cf. Eph. 1:9, emphasis added). We are saved because God extends His own lovingkindness to us.

Furthermore, despite being "dead in [our] trespasses and sins" (Eph. 2:1), God "made us alive together with Christ (by grace you have been saved)" (v. 5). Why? It is "so that in the ages to come He might show the surpassing riches of His grace *in kindness toward us* in Christ Jesus" (Eph. 2:7, emphasis added). Through His own act of salvation, God puts His loving character on display, and we are presented as trophies of His divine grace.

Similarly, in Paul's letter to Titus, we see another expression of God's kindness in salvation. We read, "But when the kindness of God our Savior and His love for mankind appeared, He saved us . . ." (Titus 3:4–5a). In this verse, we essentially see Jesus Christ as God's kindness personified. One could almost picture God's own *love* and *kindness* wrapped in the person of Jesus who comes and redeems us.[4] What a glorious picture!

The Bible teaches that the Lord Jesus Christ, who is Himself God in human flesh (John 1:1–3, 14), came to earth and lived in perfect obedience to every law of God, thus perfectly fulfilling the divine standard. Jesus lived sinlessly (2 Cor. 5:21; Heb. 4:15; 1 Peter 2:22), and thereby gave Himself up to be killed as an atoning sacrifice—a *propitiation*—for sin (1 John 2:2). Being the only acceptable sacrifice for sin, Jesus Christ died in the place of sinners as a *substitute* (1 Peter 2:24), paying a ransom to the Father; *redeeming* us from the curse of the law (Gal. 3:13).

Through the sacrificial death of Jesus, we can have our sins *forgiven* by God (Col. 2:13), and we are *justified*—declared righteous and pardoned by God, even though we're guilty and unrighteous (Rom. 3:28; Gal. 2:16). It is the work of Jesus Christ on the cross that makes the forgiveness of sin possible for us. And not only forgiveness, but *reconciliation* to God—the restoration of relationship. More than this, God actually *adopts* us as His own (Rom. 8:12–17; Gal. 4:4–7). Now, we who were formerly His enemies have now become God's children.

It is only by the death of Christ that we will find any hope of forgiveness for sin. All other attempts to "get right with God" are doomed to fail. Why? Because, by nature, we are sinful creatures, and when we try to accomplish anything of redeeming value, God turns up His nose and is repulsed by the gesture (Isa. 64:6–7). Any attempt we make to justify ourselves before Him is insulting and futile. Only the perfect work of Jesus Christ on our behalf is pleasing to the Father.

All in all, we see that God's offer of salvation to sinners is a glorious demonstration of His goodness and kindness. When we truly comprehend this truth, we can exclaim with the psalmist: "But I have trusted in Your lovingkindness; my heart shall rejoice in Your salvation. I will sing to the LORD, because He has dealt bountifully with me" (Ps. 13:5–6).

Chapter Two

GOD'S KINDNESS IN REPENTANCE AND FAITH

---

*Do you think lightly of the riches of His kindness
and tolerance and patience, not knowing that
the kindness of God leads you to repentance?* **(Rom. 2:4)**

King Nebuchadnezzar believed that he was the greatest king in the world. More than this, he believed that he himself was a god. Daniel 3 records how an image of the king was erected, and all the people were commanded to bow down and worship his image (v. 5). When three young Israelites refused, an enraged Nebuchadnezzar bound them and threw them into a fiery furnace. To his utter shock and dismay, the three boys—Shadrach, Meshach, and Abednego—were spared with the help of a fourth figure (undoubtedly the Lord!) who appeared in the fire with them (vv. 19–25). The miraculous event sobered the king and he declared that his whole kingdom was prohibited from speaking against the God of Shadrach, Meshach, and Abednego (vv. 28–29).

When we encounter Nebuchadnezzar again at the end of Daniel 4, he is pacing the roof of his palace, gloating over the marvel and expanse of his kingdom. Only he did not give glory to God but claimed all power and glory for himself. In the middle of his boasting, the Lord spoke from heaven and told him, "'King Nebuchadnezzar, to you it is declared: sovereignty has been removed from you, and you will be driven away from mankind, and your dwelling place will be with the beasts of the field'" (Dan. 4:31–32). In one divine act, Nebuchadnezzar was reduced to nothing. For the next seven years, the great king wandered around in the fields, naked and exposed, eating the grass, growing out his hair and nails, and without a sane thought in his mind.

By all accounts, Nebuchadnezzar would have wandered around like an animal until his death, but at the end of seven years, the Lord restored his mind and body, as well as his kingdom. He later recalled, "I, Nebuchadnezzar, raised my eyes toward heaven and my reason returned to me, and I blessed the Most High and praised and honored Him who lives forever" (v. 34). Once fully restored, the Babylonian king declared, "Now I, Nebuchadnezzar, praise, exalt and honor the King of heaven, for all His works are true and His ways just, and He is able to humble those who walk in pride" (v. 37). In this dramatic turnaround, we behold God's kindness in granting repentance to a once-prideful king.

What an amazing story of mercy, compassion, and restoration! The height of Nebuchadnezzar's arrogance combined with the baseness of his humiliation only magnifies God's abject kindness to him. And if God is willing to extend such undeserved goodness to a haughty tyrant, then there is hope for us as well.

GRACIOUS AND MERCIFUL

In the last chapter, we discussed how, despite humanity's free fall into sin, God offers salvation according to His lovingkindness. Out of the goodness of God's character, He provides a way of forgiveness and restoration. However, when we further plumb the depths of what we know about God, we are awestruck to find even deeper expressions of His lovingkindness to us. Namely, the extension of God's own *grace* and *mercy* toward us.

Grace and mercy work together. And both proceed from the depths of who God is. We could say that *grace* is unmerited favor, while *mercy* is undeserved forbearance. Or to put it another way, God's grace is the blessing that He gives to others that they have not earned, while His mercy is the withholding of punishment that they have earned. For example, receiving a birthday gift is an experience of pure grace—you did nothing to earn it; you were simply born—while not receiving a speeding ticket when you blew through a stop sign at seventy miles per hour is an example of mercy.

We read, "For *by grace* you have been saved through faith; and that not of yourselves, it is the gift of God" (Eph. 2:8, emphasis added). We are saved because of God's desire to bless us even though we have done nothing to deserve it.

Additionally, Romans 9 calls those who God saves "vessels of mercy, which He prepared beforehand for glory" (v. 23). Even though we were otherwise destined for wrath and punishment, God exercised mercy to withhold judgment from us.

As we have noted several times, we cannot parse out God's attributes and isolate them from one another. They all flow together out of the perfect heart of God to display His full glory. And so, it's out of God's goodness and loving-kindness that He displays His grace and mercy to us. With regard to salvation, it is not automatic. God does not save every person indiscriminately. Rather, by His own character, He grants to His people the necessary gifts that they must possess to receive the benefits of salvation. According to His own kindness, God grants *repentance* and *faith* to every person He intends to save.

FAITHFUL REPENTANCE

God is not obligated to extend His saving grace to anyone. Yet in His lovingkindness, He shows the mercy needed for the sinner to seek forgiveness. In His act of saving the sinner, God grants them the recognition of sinfulness as well as their desire to be made right with God. In other words, in order to be saved, a sinner must recognize that they have sinned against God, admit their guilt, and turn away from their wickedness through trusting in the finished work of Jesus Christ. This is what is known as *repentance*.

In the Old Testament, a word commonly used for repentance is *shub*, meaning "to change a course of action, to turn away, or to turn back."[1] The word was often used to refer to a geographical return, as in the return of God's people from exile. However, it was also used to articulate a spiritual return to God. The New Testament is dominated by the Greek word *metanoia*, which literally means "after-thought" and has to do with a change of mind. Sinclair Ferguson defines repentance as "a change of mind that leads to a change of lifestyle."[2] Or as Thomas Watson articulates: "Repentance is a grace of God's Spirit whereby a sinner is inwardly humbled and visibly reformed."[3]

In Luke 15, Jesus tells the story of the prodigal son—a beautiful picture of repentance and restoration. The son, after squandering his father's inheritance and living among pigs, has a change of mind, a change of heart. Jesus retells, "But when he came to himself" (v. 17) the son decided to return to the father and ask forgiveness. This heartfelt realization—a coming to your spiritual senses—is a surefire sign of repentance.

However, repentance is not simply something we conjure out of thin air. Thomas Brooks notes, "Repentance is a flower that grows not in nature's garden."[4] God must do a work within our hearts to produce it, but we must understand that the origin of this gift resides within God—in His goodness and kindness toward us. Israel's iniquities were pardoned "according to the greatness of [God's] loving-kindness" (Num. 14:19). In David's psalm of repentance, he pleads with the Lord to "be gracious to me, O God, according to Your lovingkindness" (Ps. 51:1). Elsewhere, he declares, "For You, Lord, are good, and ready to forgive, and abundant in lovingkindness to all who call upon You" (Ps. 86:5). The granting of repentance and forgiveness of sins is all rooted in God's own character—His goodness and lovingkindness.

Paul picked up this theme in Romans 2:4: "Or do you think lightly of the riches of His kindness and tolerance and patience, not knowing that the kindness of God leads you to repentance?" More than granting repentance to the sinner as a gift, the Bible teaches that it is the lovingkindness of God that motivates and produces repentance. How so? Thomas Watson explains, "The goodness of God is a spiritual sunbeam to melt the heart into tears."[5] When we behold the bountiful kindness of God to us, our hearts melt down and we cry out to God in repentance. As Wilhelmus à Brakel puts it, "The goodness of God is the reason why a believer, even after many backslidings, is motivated by renewal to return unto the Lord."[6]

I cannot help but think of the time when David was on the run from Saul. At one point, David has an opportunity to kill Saul in his sleep, but he spares him. Upon realizing David's own kindness and forbearance to him, the Bible says that "Saul lifted up his voice and wept" (1 Sam. 24:16). When God grants a sinner the gift of repentance, it wrenches their heart and they cry out to God. In fact, their words may echo those of David: "Do not remember the sins of my youth or my transgressions; according to Your lovingkindness remember me, for Your goodness' sake, O Lᴏʀᴅ" (Ps. 25:7).

What about you? Maybe you can recall a time when you were "on the run" from God's call and experienced a level of merciful kindness that awakened your heart and stirred you to turn away from your pursuit and back to the lovingkindness of God. For me, it was a period of time after my parents' divorce where I wandered away from the Lord. Looking back, I have referred to those years as my "desert days." But I wonder if, like me, you are deeply grateful that the Lord reached down to halt your wayward course.

As we see demonstrated with King Saul and in our own lives, genuine repentance is the result of God's lovingkindness poured out on those who need it most.

THE ELEMENTS OF REPENTANCE

Before we go too far, we should take the time to understand the various elements of repentance. How do we know that our repentance is real? Simply feeling sorry for sin is not by itself repentance. Often the knee-jerk reaction of sorrow is tied more to the fact that we have been caught and have to suffer penalty; not that one is sorry over the sin itself. And so, in order to shepherd us into a right understanding of repentance, God in His kindness has established three main elements.

The first is *intellectual*. At a certain point, a person needs to recognize that they've sinned. God's command has been transgressed and rebellion is taking place. It's a mental acknowledgment; a realization. This is what it means to "come to your senses" (cf. Luke 15:17). After all, the New Testament Greek word *metanoia* pertains mostly to the mind, as it comes to the awareness of sin and experiences a change in thinking. King David, after sinning with Bathsheba, wrote, "I acknowledged my sin to you, and I did not cover my iniquity" (Ps. 32:5 ESV). John MacArthur writes that "repentance begins with a recognition of sin—the understanding that we are sinners, that our sin is an affront to a holy God, and more precisely, that we are personally responsible for our own guilt."[7] One of the biggest problems we face is an inability, even an unwillingness, to recognize and admit our own guilt over sin. However, we must call it what it is and be prepared to follow through with what we have purposed in our mind.

The second is *emotional*. This is where the feelings enter into the equation. It's important to note that remorse over our current situation isn't necessarily a sign of true repentance, but there needs to be genuine sorrow over our sin (2 Cor. 7:9–11) and over transgressing God's law. As a Christian believer, we are right to be deeply troubled that we have offended God with our transgression. Further, we have broken communion with Him. Again, David declares to the Lord, "For you will not delight in sacrifice, or I would give it. . . . The sacrifices of God are a broken spirit; a broken and contrite heart, O God, you will not despise" (Ps. 51:16–17 ESV). God wants us broken and mourning over our sin. That is the mark of true repentance. But there is still more.

The third is *volitional*. This is an act of the will. Surely

the first step is the confession of sin; working in league with
the first part—the intellect—to realize and own up to the
sin. Louis Berkhof notes that there is "a volitional element,
consisting in a change of purpose, an inward turning away
from sin, and a disposition to seek pardon and cleansing."[8]
Repentance must always include action. Something must
change, otherwise there is no proof that the heart is being
moved toward the Lord. When King Solomon set out to
dedicate the new temple, the Lord came to him and affirmed
the promise of the covenant that if the people obeyed they
would receive divine blessing. The Lord told him, "If my
people who are called by my name humble themselves, and
pray and seek my face and *turn from their wicked ways*, then
I will hear from heaven and will forgive their sin and heal
their land" (2 Chron. 7:14, emphasis added ESV). A definite
turning must occur, otherwise there is no visible evidence of
repentance (see Matt. 3:8)!

What is God's promise to us with regard to repentance?
"If we confess our sins, he is faithful and just to forgive us our
sins and to cleanse us from all unrighteousness" (1 John 1:9
ESV). The promise is twofold: He will forgive our sins,
removing our transgressions from us (cf. Ps. 103:12; Col.
2:14); and He will cleanse us, washing us from the inside
out, restoring our souls (Ps. 51:7; Eph. 5:26–27; Titus 3:5).
While sin must be confessed because of its sheer offense to
God, He is also gracious in desiring to forgive and restore us.

It is important, however, for us to understand that repentance is only one aspect of how we receive God's gracious

gift of salvation. We must recognize our fallen condition and desire restoration before anything can take place. But the actual gift of salvation is given to us by the means of our faith.

REPENTANT FAITH

When Jesus met the Samaritan woman at a well in John 4, you can be sure that she had no idea that her life was about to change forever. Within a few minutes of talking, Jesus exposes that she has been married five times and is living in sin with another man (John 4:17–18). But in His kindness, the Lord offers her "living water" by which she "shall never thirst . . . [and] will become in [her] a well of water springing up to eternal life (vv. 10, 14). In this one encounter, Jesus both exposes her sin and offers eternal life, which she receives gratefully. She responds by confessing her sins to others ("Come, see a man who told me all the things that I have done" [v. 29]) and proclaiming Him as the long-awaited Savior—the Christ. In one encounter, the Lord grants the Samaritan woman repentant, saving faith.

Perhaps you can relate, if not with this woman's specific circumstances then with her sense of brokenness, the deep-seated and painful longing in her life. Maybe, like her, you've found yourself going about the business of everyday life—"drawing water" or commuting to work or sitting in church—when the Lord in His lovingkindness has confronted you in your waywardness, to stir you to repentance, to offer you the "living water" that is only available in knowing and walking with Him. If so, you have experienced the tender mercy of God's kindness.

When we consider the importance of repentance, we must remember that it is not actually by repentance that we are saved—it is *by faith alone in Jesus Christ* (Rom. 3:28; Gal. 2:16; Eph. 2:8–9). In fact, Richard Owen Roberts writes, "Repentance is not the entry ticket into the kingdom of God, but it is a condition of citizenship."[9] However, the link between the two is unbreakable, as "repentance and faith are wed together, never to be divorced. True repentance does not stand alone but is always linked with true faith. True faith does not stand alone but is always linked with true repentance."[10] By faith, a step away from the rebellion of sin is also a step toward obedience to God. Louis Berkhof writes,

> *True repentance never exists except in conjunction with faith, while, on the other hand, wherever there is true faith, there is also real repentance. The two are but different aspects of the same turning, . . . a turning away from sin in the direction of God . . . the two cannot be separated; they are simply complementary parts of the same process.*[11]

By faith, we recognize and trust that God is who He says He is, and what He has revealed is good, right, and true. By faith, we repent of transgressing His perfect law. By faith, we trust that what He has promised to those who obey is greater than the shortsighted kick we get from sin, as a lifetime of unrepentant sin condemns us to hell. By faith, we repent;

our repentance is a fruit of our faith. To further illustrate, Psalm 32, which is a psalm of repentance, closes with these words: "Many are the sorrows of the wicked, but he who trusts in the LORD, lovingkindness shall surround him. Be glad in the LORD and rejoice, you righteous ones; and shout for joy, all you who are upright in heart" (vv. 10–11).

Roberts is unequivocal: "Both repentance and faith are mandatory to salvation. You must turn from your sin in order to turn to Jesus Christ. You cannot turn to Christ unless you have turned from your sin. Repentance and faith belong together. Any attempt to separate them is a grievous mistake."[12] But we cannot miss the fact that, like repentance, saving faith is a gift of God given to us according to His own kindness.

GRACIOUS GIFTS TO THE UNDESERVING

In the beginning of this book, I laid out what I have been calling "the Grand Premise." To refresh our memory, it is as follows: *God is good; we are sinful. Because of this, we are undeserving of His goodness. But because of God's mercy, He demonstrates lovingkindness to us. Therefore, every kindness we experience is pure grace and ought to be received with gladness and thankfulness.* When we consider this premise in light of our discussion on repentance and faith, we are reminded that we are dead in sin (Eph. 2:1–3), and because of this, we do not deserve His goodness. And so, when we receive goodness and kindness from God, it is an expression of both His mercy and grace.

When God brings us to our senses and exposes our sin so that we confess it to Him, it is a benevolent act of kindness. God would be just to leave us in our rebellious condition. He does not owe us forgiveness for our sins or saving faith. In fact, He has every right to deliver us over to our own sinfulness and condemn us (Rom. 1:18–32). Yet He graciously grants repentance to a sinner who would otherwise harden their own hearts in rebellion. He kindly bestows faith in Jesus Christ to a selfish person who would otherwise trust only in themselves. God would redeem and save even one sinner, and it would be a tremendous act of lovingkindness! And then when we consider that God has extended such grace to countless millions throughout history, we are blown away with gladness and abundant thankfulness.

While living in a cruel world that is free-falling into destruction, we can't help but see that God's lovingkindness to grant repentance and faith isn't just life from death—it's better than life!

Chapter Three

GOD'S KINDNESS IN SANCTIFICATION

Like newborn babies, long for the pure milk of the word,
so that by it you may grow in respect to salvation,
if you have tasted the kindness of the Lord. **(1 Peter 2:2–3)**

When Jesus first met the man called Simon Barjona, he
was a simple Galilean fisherman. As a Jew, he was likely
devout, but perhaps only as much as he had to be. The day
his brother Andrew came running to him, yelling, "We have
found the Messiah!" (John 1:41) would be a day he would
never forget. When Simon met Him in person, Jesus took
one look at him and said, "You are Simon the son of John;
you shall be called Cephas (which is translated Peter)" (John
1:42). A little while later, when Jesus was walking along the
Sea of Galilee, He saw both Andrew and Peter out fishing.
When He came closer to them, He commanded them both,
"Follow Me, and I will make you fishers of men" (Matt. 4:19).
Starting at this point, Simon Peter began following Jesus.

Over the next two years, Peter traveled with Jesus and

His disciples, witnessing miracles and listening to profound teaching. He was even sent by the Lord on a short mission to bring the gospel "to the lost sheep of the house of Israel" (Matt. 10:6). Upon their eventual arrival in the district of Caesarea Philippi, Jesus seized an opportunity to ask His disciples, "Who do you say that I am?" (Matt. 16:15). Peter, no doubt responding on behalf of the disciples, confessed: "You are the Christ, the Son of the living God" (v. 16). Jesus responded joyfully: "Blessed are you, Simon Barjona, because flesh and blood did not reveal this to you, but My Father who is in heaven" (v. 17). Peter's first confession of saving faith came not from himself, but was graciously granted to him by God—an expression of profound lovingkindness. Peter was now a true believer.

Peter stayed close to Jesus' side for the whole ministry, receiving blessing upon blessing from the Lord. On the night before His death, Jesus predicts His own betrayal by the hand of Judas Iscariot, and then tells His disciples of His plans to go away (to death). Despite Peter's eager profession of faithfulness, Jesus prophesies his betrayal—"Truly, truly, I say to you, a rooster will not crow until you deny Me three times" (John 13:38). Within a matter of hours, Peter thrice denies Jesus and flees in the dark of night, weeping bitterly (John 18:25–27; cf. Matt. 26:75). After His resurrection, however, Jesus graciously gives Peter an opportunity to thrice declare his love for Him, thus forgiving and restoring him completely (John 21:15–17)—an act of lovingkindness.

By Acts 2 we see Peter as an apostle—an ambassador of

Jesus Christ—preaching to the multitudes in Jerusalem. Far from the days of his faithlessness and denial of Christ, Peter is running well and ministering faithfully. However, when Peter arrives in Antioch much later, he begins to backslide into his old Jewish ways, forsaking his newly converted Gentile brothers and sisters in Christ (Gal. 2:11–13). This causes the apostle Paul to confront him publicly, calling him to repentance (vv. 14–21). While Scripture does not record it, church history attests to the fact that God granted repentance to Peter, and he pressed on with his ministry for the next several decades.

In his final years of ministry, we see a mature believer, sanctified and strengthened by the grace and goodness of the Lord. Reflecting on his own experience with the Lord, he exhorts the persecuted believers scattered abroad:

> *Therefore, putting aside all malice and all deceit and hypocrisy and envy and all slander, like newborn babies, long for the pure milk of the word, so that by it you may grow in respect to salvation,* if you have tasted the kindness of the Lord. *(1 Peter 2:1–3, emphasis added)*

After years of growing in the Lord, Peter encourages the growth of the saints, rooting their sanctification in the kindness of God that they have experienced. While not perfect, Peter finishes the course of his life having been more conformed to the image of Jesus Christ, proclaiming the necessity for believers to "grow in the grace and knowledge of our Lord and Savior Jesus Christ" (2 Peter 3:17). Peter had experienced the grace and kindness of God, and it had transformed him, day by day, until he took his final breath.

THE NEED FOR SPIRITUAL GROWTH

We have already seen how God rescues sinners and saves them according to His own lovingkindness. In doing so, He grants them repentance and faith—both are the means by which salvation is received (e.g., Mark 1:15; Acts 2:38). However, even when we are saved from the eternal consequences of our sin, we still live in corrupted bodies with sinful minds. As Paul says, "our outer man is decaying" (2 Cor. 4:16), but he holds on to the hope that God is doing something restorative within us. What is his hope? He concludes, "Yet our inner man is being renewed day by day." To what is he referring? He is speaking about the divine process of *sanctification*.

In his first letter to the Thessalonians, Paul declared in no uncertain terms: "For this is the will of God, your sanctification" (4:3). What is *sanctification*? While there are a few different uses for the word in the Bible, we understand generally that it is the process of becoming holy, set apart or separated, consecrated to God. With regard to our present experience of sanctification in this life, Wayne Grudem defines it as "a progressive work of God and man that makes us more and more free from sin and like Christ in our actual lives."[1] In the context of the Bible, it is the process of separating from sin and worldliness, and growing in holiness and godliness. Furthermore, it consists of our growing conformity to Jesus Christ in thought, word, and deed (Rom. 8:29; 12:2). In fact, Paul told the Corinthian church to "be imitators of me, just as I also am of Christ" (1 Cor. 11:1). Similarly, we are called to "be imitators of God, as beloved children" (Eph. 5:1).

Sadly, there are common misconceptions regarding the nature of our spiritual growth in holiness (sanctification). Jerry Bridges writes that "holiness is not a series of do's and don'ts, but conformity to the character of God and obedience to the will of God."[2] In essence, we are trying to be like the Lord, who is Himself represented to us perfectly in Jesus Christ (Col. 1:15; Heb. 1:3). Once again, we are told, "But put on the Lord Jesus Christ, and make no provision for the flesh, to gratify its desires" (Rom. 13:14 ESV).

In Ephesians 4, the apostle Paul introduced the church to a principle of sanctification, whereby the believer is to "put off your old self, which belongs to your former manner of life and is corrupt through deceitful desires" (v. 22 ESV); and, in its place, "put on the new self, created after the likeness of God in true righteousness and holiness" (v. 24 ESV). This two-handed approach to sanctification—the "put off/put on" principle—is what is prescribed for growing in godliness.

In applying Paul's method, the believer is called to identify and confess sin, while praying for God to help root out and replace it with the corresponding fruit of the Spirit (Gal. 5:22–23). For example, in the case of slandering another person, confess the sin and ask God to help find ways to build that person up and exhort them. In the case of pride and self-righteousness, confess the sin and enlist the help of the Lord to teach you the ways of humility.

I remember meeting with a young couple in our church who were living together outside of marriage. While they both loved each other and wanted to grow together in the Lord, I shared with them from the Scriptures that their decision to have premarital sex was actually an act of rebellion against the commands of God (e.g., Eph. 5:3; 1 Thess. 4:3; Heb. 13:4; etc.). Once they realized that they were living in sin, they repented to the Lord and asked for forgiveness. Immediately, the young man moved out of the couple's bedroom until they were married a few weeks later. Since then, the Lord has blessed their obedience by giving them both a vibrant faith, a strong marriage, and a house full of children.

Living a godly life is not optional. Growing in Christlikeness is not optional. In fact, Jesus Himself tells His disciples that if their lives are not bearing the fruit of righteousness, it is evidence that they do not belong to Him and will eventually be cut off and thrown into the fire (John 15:1–8)! The author of Hebrews tells us that we are to "pursue peace with all men, *and the sanctification without which no one will see the Lord*" (Heb. 12:14, emphasis added). Did you catch that? If you are not chasing after holiness in your Christian walk, you will have no chance of seeing the Lord in eternity. Why? Because you will prove that your faith is not genuine (James 2:14–17).

We cannot afford to be spiritually lazy. Paul described the

Christian life as a race and a boxing match (1 Cor. 9:24–27). It's a life that will be marked with trials and suffering. But we are encouraged: "Since therefore Christ suffered in the flesh, arm yourselves with the same way of thinking, for whoever has suffered in the flesh has ceased from sin, so as to live for the rest of the time in the flesh no longer for human passions but for the will of God" (1 Peter 4:1–2 ESV). We must be contenders for the faith (Jude 1:3), those who labor tirelessly for goodness, righteousness, and holiness. Writing about the challenge of striving for holiness, J. C. Ryle notes,

> *There are thousands of men and women who go to churches and chapels every Sunday, and call themselves Christians. Their names are in the baptismal register. They are reckoned Christians while they live. They are married with a Christian marriage service. They mean to be buried as Christians when they die. But you never see any "fight" about their religion! Of spiritual strife and exertion and conflict and self-denial and watching and warring they know literally nothing at all.*[3]

Now, at this point, you might start to feel a bit overwhelmed. *I'm not so sure I can do this! I don't know if I'm strong enough!* When we consider the idea of confronting our sins and daily striving to be like Christ, the task feels insurmountable. Thankfully, our sanctification is also a gift of the Lord—a gracious and continuous work of the Spirit within us to conform us to the image of Christ.

OUR SANCTIFICATION BY THE LORD

Writing to the Philippians, the apostle Paul exhorted them to live with one another in joy and unity, looking to Christ as the ultimate example of selflessness (Phil. 2:1–8). Following his marvelous declaration of the exaltation and glory of Christ in verses 9–11 ("God highly exalted Him, and bestowed on Him the name which is above every name, so that at the name of Jesus every knee will bow . . . and that every tongue will confess that Jesus Christ is Lord, to the glory of God the Father."), Paul exhorted believers to action. He told them in verse 12, "So then, my beloved, just as you have always obeyed, not as in my presence only, but now much more in my absence, work out your salvation with fear and trembling."

Philippians 2:12 has been met with much confusion over the years. Read a certain way, the verse almost seems to imply that we are saved by our own works ("work out your salvation with fear and trembling"). However, we know that this cannot be the natural meaning of this verse because it would contradict the countless other verses in Scripture that attribute our salvation to the Lord, and not to our own works (e.g., John 1:12–13; Rom. 3:28; Gal. 2:16; Eph. 2:8–9; etc.). Therefore, the verse must be teaching something else.

The context of verse 12 is the *obedience* to the Lord that is required of all believers. In other words, we are called to grow in holiness and in sanctification. In hedging against spiritual laziness, Paul essentially exhorted believers to "work

out [the fruit of] your salvation with fear and trembling."
How do we know that this is what Paul meant? How do we
know that this work is not completely accomplished by the
believer? Because of verse 13: "for it is God who is at work
in you, both to will and to work for His good pleasure."
Elsewhere, we are told that God has prepared beforehand
abundant good works in which we are to walk (Eph. 2:10).
Even though God commands us to live lives of obedience
to Him, by His own kindness, He Himself is the One who
works within us to bring our sanctification to fruition.

How does God accomplish this?

By the Spirit

Once we have been redeemed and saved by Jesus Christ,
God does not leave us alone to do the rest. I've heard this
popular adage for years: "God has done His part [salvation],
now you have to do your part [sanctification]." However, the
Bible does not describe spiritual growth this way. One of the
errors of the Galatian Christians was their belief that, once
they had been saved, they had to flip a switch and engage in
spiritual disciplines by their own human effort. Paul rebuked
them, "Are you so foolish? Having begun by the Spirit, are
you now being perfected by the flesh?" (Gal. 3:3). The question is rhetorical; the answer is no. All of our Christian life is
to be lived *by the Spirit*. How so?

In John 14, Jesus told His disciples that once He went
away, the Father would send "another Helper" who would
"be with you forever" (v. 16). He then called Him "the Spirit

of truth," with whom the world will not be acquainted. However, Jesus promised not only that the Spirit would be *with* them, but also *in* them. We see the fulfillment of this in Acts 2:1–4 at Pentecost. We understand this to be the indwelling presence of the Holy Spirit within the heart of every believer.

Once the Spirit indwells a Christian believer at salvation —having believed "the message of truth, the gospel of your salvation"—we are "sealed . . . with the Holy Spirit of promise" (Eph. 1:13). He applies the finished work of Christ to us in salvation, binding us to Him forever, and stamps us with a heavenly seal, marking us out as the prized possession of the Lord (Titus 2:14; 1 Peter 2:9). The presence of the Holy Spirit within us proves the irremovable work of God to save and redeem us for all eternity.

Once within us, however, the Spirit also sanctifies us (Rom. 15:16; 1 Cor. 6:11; 1 Peter 1:2; etc.). He strives with us to conform us to the image of Christ. He convicts us of our sins (John 16:8). He helps us to root out sins and put them to death (Rom. 8:13). He gives us wisdom, under-standing, and spiritual illumination of the things revealed to us in Scripture (1 Cor. 2:6–16). He produces in us the fruit of righteousness—love, joy, peace, patience, *kindness*, good-ness, faithfulness, gentleness, self-control (Gal. 5:22–23, emphasis added). It is by the indwelling and sanctifying ministry of the Holy Spirit that "God . . . is at work in you, both to will and to work for His good pleasure" (Phil. 2:13).

By the Word

Another means by which God extends kindness to us in sanctification is through giving us His word. John 1 calls Jesus Christ "the Word." He is the eternal embodiment of God's divine revelation. However, in the course of history, God has revealed His truth to us through the written word—the Bible. We receive the Scriptures by divine inspiration—they're "God-breathed" (2 Tim. 3:16) and profitable to help us in order that we may be "equipped for every good work" (v. 17). Did you catch that? God gave us the Bible, not only to reveal divine information to us, but also to help us to live godly lives.

In John 17, Jesus prays to the Father on behalf of His disciples. Initially, He is concerned about their preservation —that they may be kept from the evil one (v. 15). But His thoughts quickly turn to the need for them all to grow spiritually. And so, He prays in verse 17, "Sanctify them in the truth; Your word is truth." Jesus not only prays for this, but He *knows* that sanctification cannot happen apart from God's Word.

In many places in Scripture, we see the connection between God's own kindness and the revelation of His Word. In fact, Solomon prays for his son: "Do not let kindness and truth leave you; bind them around your neck, write them on the tablet of your heart" (Prov. 3:3). The psalmist notes the importance of learning the Word of God. He writes, "The earth is full of Your lovingkindness, O LORD; teach me Your statutes" (Ps. 119:64). Furthermore, he understands that

God's Word will bring revival to his soul: "Revive me according to Your lovingkindness, so that I may keep the testimony of Your mouth" (v. 88; cf. Ps. 119:149). Once again, the psalmist connects God's kindness and truth: "Deal with Your servant according to Your lovingkindness and teach me Your statutes" (v. 124). God's word reveals His lovingkindness to His people.

I've often pondered the fact that God could have remained silent. He didn't have to give us the Bible. He could have created us and let us wander around aimlessly, trying to figure out what to do to please Him (think: Greek gods). However, He didn't do that! In kindness, He patiently and painstakingly spent sixteen hundred years progressively revealing His purposes and plans for us. Through the revelation of Jesus Christ to us, we have been granted "everything pertaining to life and godliness, through the true knowledge of Him who called us by His own glory and excellence" (2 Peter 1:3). Furthermore, we have all we need, bound up in the Scriptures, to live sanctified lives and engage in good works.

Through Prayer

A Christian's sanctification is a work of the Holy Spirit, which is informed and empowered by the word of God. However, it is a work of God within us in which we participate. It's not that *we* make ourselves more holy—only God can do that. But we labor and strive *alongside* the Spirit in full obedience to the Lord. And as we draw closer to God, the primary way that we express our faith, desire, and dependence on Him is through prayer.

Jesus told His disciples that they were to "pray that [they] may not enter into temptation" (Luke 22:40; cf. Matt. 6:13). In this way, prayer is our defensive weapon so that we don't stumble into sinfulness. This is why Paul told the church in Ephesus, "With all prayer and petition pray at all times in the Spirit, and with this in view, be on the alert with all perseverance and petition for all the saints" (Eph. 6:18).

We also read about Paul's prayers for believers to receive spiritual illumination (Eph. 1:18) and wisdom (Col. 1:9–10). With regard to sanctification and growth, Jude commends believers: "But you, beloved, building yourselves up on your most holy faith, praying in the Holy Spirit, keep yourselves in the love of God, waiting anxiously for the mercy of our Lord Jesus Christ to eternal life" (Jude 1:20–21). Again, there is no intrinsic power in our prayers, but it is the act of leaning on the Lord who accomplishes all things that is truly powerful. This is why we are commanded to "pray without ceasing" (1 Thess. 5:17).

But what if we are struggling to pray? We may understand the need to grow spiritually, but there are times when we can feel like we just can't even take a step forward or ask the Lord for help. However, we are encouraged to read that, "In the same way the Spirit also helps our weakness; for we do not know how to pray as we should, but the Spirit Himself intercedes for us with groanings too deep for words; and He who searches the hearts knows what the mind of the Spirit is, because He intercedes for the saints according to the will of God" (Rom. 8:26–27). Even when we don't even know what to do, God demonstrates His lovingkindness to us by the Spirit's intercession and ministry of prayer. He helps us pray! What immeasurable kindness!

PREPARING US FOR GLORY

As we have seen, this whole ministry of divine sanctification is one of immense kindness. God did not have to give us the Spirit, but He did so out of His lovingkindness. He did not have to give us His Word, but He did so out of His lovingkindness. He did not have to open up a direct line to His own heart through prayer, but He did so out of His lovingkindness.

Why is God so invested in our sanctification? The Bible teaches that there is coming a day when every Christian will pass away and leave this sinful dwelling behind. Our bodies will die, and when our eyes open up in heaven, we will be changed (1 Cor. 15:52). The apostle John spoke of this when he wrote, "Beloved, now we are children of God, and it has not appeared as yet what we will be. We know that when He appears, we will be like Him, because we will see Him just as He is. And everyone who has this hope fixed on Him purifies himself, just as He is pure" (1 John 3:2–3). In other words, the Bible tells us that we will see Jesus face-to-face, and when we do, we will have been perfected like Him.

Therefore, when we consider that sanctification is the process of making us more like Christ, the completion of that process is glorification in heaven with Christ. If this is true, then on the most basic and practical level, our sanctification now on earth is the process of God preparing us for the glories of heaven. He takes special care to cleanse us and purge us from the defilement of sin so that He may present us to Himself in the future (cf. Eph. 5:27). Behold God's tender and loving care for us! Consider His gracious kindness to change us from the inside out! Even though the process of sanctification can be painful, we know that the final result will be that we will see His holiness. For without sanctification, we will never see the Lord (Heb. 12:14).

Chapter Four

GOD'S KINDNESS IN RELATIONSHIPS

---

*"Greater love has no one than this, that one
lay down his life for his friends."* **(John 15:13)**

There is a high cost to following Jesus Christ. The disciples had experienced this firsthand. He had told them in Luke 14:26, "If anyone comes to Me, and does not hate his own father and mother and wife and children and brothers and sisters, yes, even his own life, he cannot be My disciple." Naturally, they all understood that Jesus was speaking hyperbolically—He was not commanding them to truly hate anyone. In fact, Jesus had instructed them, "Love your enemies and pray for those who persecute you" (Matt. 5:44).

But His point was crystal clear. It was about allegiance. None of the disciples were permitted to affix their hearts to any*one* or any*thing*—they were to devote themselves completely to the Lord. And this seriousness of devotion to Christ would appear to be almost hatred of others by comparison. Furthermore, Jesus also told them that following

Him would elicit hatred from others (Matt. 10:22), even from members of their own families (Matt. 10:36).

At one point during their mission, Peter lamented to the Lord, "Behold, we have left everything and followed You" (Mark 10:28). No doubt speaking on behalf of all the disciples, Peter expressed his deep concern that they would ultimately lose everything and become impoverished (cf. Matt. 19:27). Jesus' response to the complaint was not one of indignation—*Oh you of little faith; don't be so greedy!*—but one of encouragement. He offered this promise:

> *"Truly I say to you, there is no one who has left house or brothers or sisters or mother or father or children or farms, for My sake and for the gospel's sake, but that he will receive a hundred times as much now in the present age, houses and brothers and sisters and mothers and children and farms, along with persecutions; and in the age to come, eternal life." (vv. 29–30)*

Jesus' promise is both encouraging and intriguing. He conceded that the disciples have lost much to follow Him, both materially and relationally. Peter, Andrew, James, and John had walked away from their fishing businesses. Matthew abandoned his lucrative tax-collecting franchise. No doubt many of them angered parents and friends along the way. Of course, even Jesus Himself was at odds with the members of His own family (cf. Mark 3:20–21; John 7:5). Yet Jesus promised that they would receive back *more* than they had lost. How much more? "A hundred times as much,"

He told them. How is He able to promise all of this? It is because He is the Lord and delights to bless His people with good things.

So often today, we lament all that we *don't* have, or all that we have lost, much like Jesus' disciples did. We tend to complain against the Lord, yet do not see all of the ways He demonstrates His kindness to us. In the next chapter, we will explore a few of the ways that God blesses us materially ("houses," "farms," etc.). But in this chapter, we will take a look at how the Lord has granted to His people personal relationships as an expression of His kindness to us.

MARRIAGE

After He created the heavens and the earth, "God saw all that He had made, and behold, it was very good" (Gen. 1:31). The first time He declared that something is *not* good, however, is when He observed that the man that He had created was alone and did not have "a helper suitable for him" (Gen. 2:20). Therefore, the Lord created a woman from the side of the man and brought her to him in the world's first marriage ceremony (Gen. 2:22–25). Jesus even made reference to this blessed union when He told the Pharisees— who sinfully desired to divorce their wives "for any reason at all" (Matt. 19:3)—"So they are no longer two, but one flesh. What therefore God has joined together, let no man separate" (v. 6).

Not only does God command husbands and wives to

stay committed to one another (cf. Mal. 2:16), we are to understand that marriage is a tremendous blessing and an expression of God's kindness to us. After all, Proverbs 18:22 says, "He who finds a wife finds a good thing and obtains favor from the Lord." In fact, Abraham's servant prayed to the Lord to help him find a wife for Isaac: "O LORD, the God of my master Abraham, please grant me success today, *and show lovingkindness* to my master Abraham" (Gen. 24:12, emphasis added). And in lovingkindness, God provided Rebekah for a wife, to Isaac's great joy and delight (Gen. 24:67).

Yet so many people today seem to be down on marriage. How many times do we hear spouses referred to as "the ol' ball and chain"? Even among believers, it is not uncommon to hear people complaining about their spouse, as if God was somehow withholding kindness to them in the arrangement. But the Bible extols and lifts up marriage as a tremendous blessing! While we could no doubt identify countless blessings of marriage found in Scripture, for the moment let's focus on at least a few.

First, the blessing of marriage in *companionship*. As mentioned earlier, God created marriage to solve the problem of loneliness (Gen. 2:18). In kindness, God created for Adam "a helper suitable for him"—a woman created *from* his side who would remain with him *by* his side. Marriage serves a tremendous need for intimate interpersonal communication and loving fellowship. A loving spouse meets the need that hobbies and pets simply cannot fully satisfy. Marriage can serve as a God-given remedy for the challenge of loneliness.

Second, the blessing of marriage in *sanctification*. A lot of people get married because they believe that it will make them happy. And while there is certainly a large measure of happiness and joy to be found in marriage, we also see that the Lord has greater purposes for this blessed institution.[1] In a Christian marriage, God has brought together two sinners who have been redeemed through the blood of Christ. However, as both husband and wife live their lives together, their sins become more pronounced as their spouse gets a front-row seat to their flaws, struggles, and sinful bents. But God uses spouses to lovingly confront and minister to us in order to drive us closer to the Lord (e.g., 1 Cor. 7:14; 1 Peter 3:1–2).

Third, the blessing of marriage in *gratification*. While God intends marriage to meet our needs of companionship and spiritual growth, He has also created marriage to be a conduit of great joy and personal gratification. In addition to the joy of marital friendship and partnership, there is also the blessing of intimacy and sexual gratification. In fact, the Bible explicitly commands that all sexual activity be confined to the marriage bed (1 Cor. 7:2–5; Heb. 13:4), yet this also serves to intensify our pleasure, as all of our desires are channeled to the one with whom God has lovingly joined us together. When we experience one of the most pleasurable human experiences ever given, we ought to remember the One who created it and give Him thanks for His kindness.

Fourth, the blessing of marriage in *procreation*. While sexual activity is no doubt a source of marital pleasure, it has another crucial function. It gives us children! It grows families. We ought to praise the Lord when we consider that His command to "be fruitful and multiply, and fill the earth" (Gen. 1:28) could have been accomplished in any way He chose! Yet it is through a pleasurable act of love that God gives us our children. May we rightly praise God for His abundant kindnesses to us through the blessing of marriage.

CHILDREN AND FAMILY

In Genesis 29, we read about Jacob's agreement to work for Laban for the hand of his daughter, Rachel, in marriage. However, Laban deceived Jacob and gave him his other daughter, Leah, who was not as desirable as her sister (v. 17a). While he eventually married Rachel, the Bible tells us that, because of Jacob's preference for Rachel, he neglected Leah. We read, "Now the Lord saw that Leah was unloved, and He opened her womb" (v. 31). Despite feeling dejected and unloved by her husband, Leah received the kindness of God through bearing six sons to Jacob (vv. 32–35; 30:17, 19). As a result of receiving the blessing of children, Leah confessed, "God has endowed me with a good gift; now my husband will dwell with me, because I have borne him six sons" (30:20). In a very real and tangible way, Leah's children were the fruit of God's lovingkindness to her, even in the face of her husband's lovelessness.

Psalm 127:3 teaches us, "Behold, children are a gift of the Lord, the fruit of the womb is a reward." Sadly, some in our culture today look down on children, even seeing them as a burden or an inconvenience. But the Lord manifests a deep love for children. We read in Matthew 19:13–15 of children trying to come to Jesus who were prohibited. Jesus responded, "Let the children alone, and do not hinder them from coming to Me; for the kingdom of heaven belongs to such as these." Mark notes that, after Jesus said this, "He took them in His arms and began blessing them, laying His hands on them" (Mark 10:16). It is important that we understand how the Lord regards our children, in order that we may also see them with the right set of eyes.

When we consider the sheer miracle of life—what it takes to bring a child into the world—we marvel. (I've watched the birth of all three of my children and I still can't fathom how they got here, apart from God's own grace and kindness!) However, the Lord also charges us with the great responsibility of stewarding the gifts that He has given to us. The Bible calls us to teach and train our children (Deut. 6:4–9; Prov. 22:6), discipline them lovingly (Eph. 6:4; cf. Prov. 13:24), yet not to frustrate or exasperate them (Col. 3:21). If we fail to see our children the way God does, we will likely abdicate our responsibility and run the risk of spurning them. But if we rightly consider our children as gifts of God's kindness to us, we will respond in godly, loving, and obedient ways.

In addition to our children, the Lord also blesses us with other immediate and extended family—fathers, mothers, brothers, sisters, grandparents, cousins, uncles, aunts, nieces, nephews, and so on. Even if a person does not have children or a spouse, they are likely blessed with family. While there are times when familial relationships are shallow or even contentious, there are many times when a person's own grandparent is like that of a natural parent, or a cousin is as close as a sibling. Even when there are deficiencies in other relationships, it is not uncommon to experience the blessing of family through our other relatives. This, too, is a kindness of God to us.

THE CHURCH

There are times when a person, either through tragedy or strife, loses their connection to their natural family. This is all too common with Christians who experience a measure of persecution and rejection from their family. This was the disciples' lament to Jesus when they considered how much they had lost to follow Him. But Jesus reassured them that they would receive "a hundred times as much now in the present age . . . brothers and sisters and mothers and children" (Mark 10:29–30). Despite losing their natural family members, Jesus promised not only mere replacements but an abundance of relationships.

Just like a human body has many parts or "members," the Bible describes the church as "the body of Christ" which "has many members" (1 Cor. 12:12, 27), and that we are all "members of one another" (Eph. 4:25). In this way, the Bible describes our unity and reliance on one another. In the same way, we also see the church described as "God's household" (Eph. 2:19; 1 Tim. 3:15)—in other words, we are members of God's family. All Christians are likened to spiritual siblings. The Bible repeatedly refers to believers as "brothers" and "sisters" to one another (e.g., Rom. 14:15; 1 Cor. 1:1; 6:6; 2 Thess. 3:15; 1 Tim. 5:1; James 2:15). This closeness of spiritual family is the blessedness of Christian fellowship—a kindness of God given to all Christian believers to share with one another.

In addition to referring to us as spiritual siblings to one another, the Bible also treats more mature men and women as spiritual parents, younger believers as spiritual children. For example, Paul told the Corinthians: "For in Christ Jesus I became your father through the gospel" (1 Cor. 4:15). Writing to the believers in Thessalonica, Paul told them, "We proved to be gentle among you, as a nursing mother tenderly cares for her own children" and "were exhorting and encouraging and imploring each one of you as a father would his own children" (1 Thess. 2:7, 11). Timothy, who Paul refers to as his "true child in the faith" (1 Tim. 1:2) and "beloved son" (2 Tim. 1:2), was said to have ministered to the Corinthian church in Paul's place, having "served [him] in the furtherance of the gospel like a child serving his father" (Phil. 2:22). All of this denotes a discipling relationship, whereby older, more mature believers are helping younger believers to grow in their faith.

Building on the metaphor of spiritual family, Paul taught that we are to regard older Christian men as fathers, "younger men as brothers, the older women as mothers, and the younger women as sisters, in all purity" (1 Tim. 5:1–2). We are to see one another in this way, as spiritual family. And even if we are deprived of the blessing of natural family members, Jesus has promised to give us "a hundred times . . . brothers and sisters and mothers and children" (Mark 10:30). How is it that the Lord provides this blessing? Through His church. What an immeasurable kindness!

GOD HIMSELF

Throughout this chapter we have seen how God demonstrates His kindness through blessing us with an array of human relationships: spouses, children, natural family, and spiritual family. However, the greatest gift of kindness is that He grants to us a relationship with Himself.

While the Bible continually speaks of God's relationship to us as Creator (Gen. 1:1; Ps. 8:3–8; Eph. 3:9), Sovereign Lord (Lev. 11:44; Deut. 6:4–5; Ps. 89:8–13; Jer. 32:17), and almighty God (Gen. 17:1; Ps. 91:1–2), we know Him more intimately as our heavenly Father (Isa. 63:16–17; Matt. 6:9; Eph. 4:6). He tells us that that's who He is and invites us to come to Him as children (Rom. 8:15–17).

Not only does He love us as our Father, but He also disciplines us as children (Heb. 12:5–11) in order "that we may share His holiness" (v. 10). Even if we may not have good relationships with our own fathers and mothers, we are adopted by a perfect Father who meets our needs, protects us, loves us, and desires to be with us. Scripture proclaims: "Blessed be the God and Father of our Lord Jesus Christ, who has blessed us with every spiritual blessing in the heavenly places in Christ" (Eph. 1:3). While some may not have been especially blessed by their earthly fathers, our heavenly Father has "blessed us with every spiritual blessing"—this includes the blessing of knowing the only true God.

In addition to knowing God as our Father, we also have been blessed to have a relationship with the Son of God, the Lord Jesus Christ. Through His death on the cross and glorious resurrection, we have life and salvation in Him. He is our Savior (e.g., Eph. 5:23; Titus 2:13) and Lord (e.g., John 20:28; Rom. 7:25). However, we see an intimate relationship granted to us. In John 15, Jesus told the disciples, "Greater love has no one than this, that one lay down his life for his friends" (v. 13). And then He added, "You are My friends if you do what I command you" (v. 14). That's who Jesus is to us—He is our friend, the friend of redeemed sinners (cf. Luke 7:34).

In addition to knowing Jesus Christ as our friend, the Bible even teaches that He regards us as His spiritual siblings—brothers and sisters (e.g., Matt. 12:48–50; John 20:17). In fact, Romans 8:29 teaches that God foreknew us and predestined us "to become conformed to the image of His Son, so that He would be the firstborn among many brethren." This does not mean that we become gods with Him; we don't share in His divinity with Him. However, in our closeness of relationship, "He is not ashamed to call [us] brethren" (Heb. 2:11). Yes, Jesus is Lord, God, and Savior, but in His kindness, He extends Himself to us in ways in which we can be comforted—as a brother and a friend.

Not only is Christ our comforter, He also assured the disciples prior to His departure, "I will ask the Father, and He will give you another Helper, that He may be with you forever" (John 14:16). Some translations render this title as "Comforter"—one who comes alongside to aid us. We understand that we are comforted by God (2 Cor. 1:3) in order that we may comfort others (v. 4). But even in His ministry to us, "the Spirit Himself testifies with our spirit that we are children of God" (Rom. 8:16). Why is this important? Because we experience the cruelty of the world, our own flesh, and the devil—cruelty that tries to destroy our hope and peace. We are torn down and, in moments of weakness, we believe the lie that God has abandoned us. But the Spirit testifies to us that we belong to God.

"The Spirit also helps our weakness," says Romans 8:26, "for we do not know how to pray as we should, but the Spirit Himself intercedes for us with groanings too deep for words." He intercedes for us; He prays for us. Even if others in our life are cruel and do not comfort, He is kind. Even if others forget to pray for us, the Spirit prays for us! And even if we feel like we are all alone in this world, we have the eternal God—the triune God—who ministers to us in remarkable lovingkindness. And while we may sometimes feel like our lives are not complete unless we have a multitude of people around us, we are reminded:

*We are taught by faith to know that all the
goodness which we need and which we
ourselves lack is in God and in his Son, our
Lord Jesus Christ, in whom the Father has
placed all bounty of his blessing and grace,
so that we may all draw from him as from a
most plentiful spring.*[2]

How beautiful a thought! The only true relationship we
need is with God. Even if the Lord was all we had, He would
be enough. And yet, in His kind provision, He promises that
we will receive "a hundred times as much now in the present
age . . . brothers and sisters and mothers and children . . .
and in the age to come, eternal life" (Mark 10:30).

Chapter Five

GOD'S KINDNESS IN BLESSING

Our fathers in Egypt did not understand Your wonders;
They did not remember Your abundant kindnesses, but
rebelled by the sea, at the Red Sea. **(Ps. 106:7)**

If God told you that you were allowed to ask Him for anything, what would you request? This happened to King David's son, Solomon. The Bible tells us, "Now Solomon loved the LORD, walking in the statutes of his father David, except he sacrificed and burned incense on the high places" (1 Kings 3:3).[1] On a trip to Gibeon to offer sacrifices—a thousand of them!—the Lord appeared to him in a dream and said to him, "Ask what you wish Me to give you" (v. 5). What a strange and wonderful blessing to bestow!

What should Solomon ask for? He then prayed to the Lord, "You have shown great lovingkindness to Your servant David my father, according as he walked before You in truth and righteousness and uprightness of heart toward You; and You have reserved for him this great lovingkindness, that

You have given him a son to sit on his throne, as it is this day" (v. 6). He noted God's own demonstration of loving-kindness to David yet struggled to know what to ask for (v. 7). And so, in humility, Solomon asked for God to give him wisdom and spiritual discernment (v. 9). More than money, possessions, or fame, Solomon sought God's wisdom.

In response to his remarkable request, we read, "It was pleasing in the sight of the Lord that Solomon had asked this thing" (v. 10). Not only did God grant Solomon's request for wisdom, giving him "a wise and discerning heart" (v. 12); He also pledged to give him material wealth and great honor. In His act of kindness to Solomon, God demonstrated that He is "able to do far more abundantly beyond all that we ask or think" (Eph. 3:20). As we continue to explore various expressions of God's kindness to us, we turn our attention to how God blesses us through natural, material, providential, and supernatural means.

OUR NATURAL GIFTS AND ABILITIES

One of the most amazing things to consider about the creation of humanity is that we are made in God's image and according to His likeness (Gen. 1:26–27). This is what theologians call the *imago Dei*—the image of God. Not that we are made to resemble Him physically nor share in all His supernatural faculties, but something of God's character is imprinted on our souls. We share some of God's own attributes (known as God's *communicable attributes*). Like God, for example, we possess the ability to think and to reason; to exercise wisdom and discernment; to pursue justice and fairness; to love and to be kind.

Of course, even in our humanity, God has blessed us richly with natural abilities. I always enjoy reading about notable figures in history who were at the top of their game—people who were able to use their God-given aptitude and ability to do amazing things. These are the Einsteins and da Vincis and Augustines of the world. However, in His immeasurable kindness, God grants all of humanity with great mental faculties and natural abilities. And while most of us are not geniuses, we ought to praise the Lord that He gives us the ability to think and speak and reason and create and express and problem-solve. Without these gifts of kindness, we would not be able to live our lives with any level of success.

In addition to our mental and natural abilities, we were also given remarkable bodies. Have you ever noticed that what seemed to be impossible for humans to achieve decades ago seems almost commonplace today? Even in extraordinary feats, we keep pushing the limits of what our bodies can do. For example, on May 6, 1954, British athlete Roger Bannister became the first person in history to run a four-minute mile. Up to that point, the feat seemed impossible. Once the record had been beat, however, fifteen other runners would accomplish the same amazing feat soon thereafter[2]—and today the world record is seventeen seconds faster than Bannister's time![3]

The Bible encourages us to worship God for how He has made us. In a cascade of praise, David glorified the Lord for His amazing handiwork in creating the human form:

> *For You formed my inward parts;*
> *You wove me in my mother's womb.*
> *I will give thanks to You, for I am fearfully and*
>   *wonderfully made;*
> *Wonderful are Your works,*
> *And my soul knows it very well.*
> *My frame was not hidden from You,*
> *When I was made in secret,*
> *And skillfully wrought in the depths of the*
>   *earth;*
> *Your eyes have seen my unformed substance;*
> *And in Your book were all written*
> *The days that were ordained for me,*
> *When as yet there was none of them.*
> *(Ps. 139:13–16)*

And yet, unlike David, we tend to take our bodies and minds for granted. Or worse, we complain that we are not smarter, more physically able, or more attractive. (Even as I type this, my finger is throbbing because I dislocated it earlier today.) But our physical bodies, natural gifts, intellect, and abilities are tremendous kindnesses from God—all to be used for His glory. Even if God gave us nothing else in this world, the gift of our humanity is something to be thankful for.

OUR BASIC NEEDS

In the previous chapter we looked at the disciples' concerns for their relational and physical well-being. No doubt speaking for the group, Peter cried, "Behold, we have left everything and followed You" (Mark 10:28). Based on Jesus' response, he certainly had in mind both the loss of personal relationships as well as potential wealth that they would have earned had they stayed working their normal jobs. But Jesus promised that, despite their temporal sacrifices, they would "receive a hundred times as much now in the present age," not only "brothers and sisters and mothers and children," but also "houses . . . and farms" (v. 30). By including these items in His list, the Lord intended to comfort them with the knowing that He would meet their needs.

When the Israelites were delivered out of bondage in Egypt through the Red Sea, it was not long before they began to grumble and complain to Moses about the Lord's seeming lack of care for their needs (Ex. 16:2). Instead of punishing them for their ungratefulness, however, the Lord demonstrated His kindness by providing daily bread and meat for them, thus sustaining them for the entirety of their wilderness wandering. Yet the Israelites still complained. The psalmist even lamented their grumbling, confessing to the Lord, "Our fathers in Egypt did not understand Your wonders; *they did not remember Your abundant kindnesses*, but rebelled by the sea, at the Red Sea" (Ps. 106:7, emphasis added).

But God by His goodness and lovingkindness extended grace to His people, regularly providing for their basic needs.

In the same way He fed the Israelites, the Lord provided bread and meat for His prophet Elijah by means of ravens (1 Kings 17:4–7). In the New Testament, Jesus miraculously provided bread for thousands (cf. Matt. 14:15–21; 15:32–38). By His own character, God supplied the needs of His people. In a tender example of thanksgiving, Naomi praised God for providing through a man named Boaz, saying, "May he be blessed of the LORD who has not withdrawn his kindness to the living and to the dead" (Ruth 2:20). Boaz's kindness was a reflection of God's own kindness to them.

In His Sermon on the Mount, Jesus taught on the persistent human problem of worrying about our daily lives. He instructed His disciples, "For this reason I say to you, do not be worried about your life, as to what you will eat or what you will drink; nor for your body, as to what you will put on. Is not life more than food, and the body more than clothing?" (Matt. 6:25). Sadly, that becomes a gripe for many—grumbling about our circumstances. Yet the Lord offers this corrective: "For the Gentiles [unbelievers] eagerly seek all these things; for your heavenly Father knows that you need all these things. But seek first His kingdom and His righteousness, and all these things will be added to you" (vv. 32–33).

Do you ever doubt God's goodness to you? Do you question His kindness? Consider how He provides for your daily needs. You likely have a place to sleep at night and food to eat. Maybe sometimes it feels like you're being fed hand to mouth by ravens, but He still cares for you and meets your needs. He does not do this for billions of people because He owes it to them, but because of His goodness and lovingkindness.

GREATER MATERIAL BLESSINGS

Beyond meeting our basic needs, the Lord also frequently provides greater material blessings to people. He grants great wealth to some. In fact, we even see very wealthy believers in the Bible, such as Abraham, David, Solomon, Job, Barnabas, and others. Even today, there are many Christians who are millionaires, perhaps even billionaires.

However, most people are not considered wealthy by normal standards. Yet for those who live in the West, we are surely more materially prosperous than many who are impoverished around the world. But in moments of weakness, we can fall into the trap of doubting God's kindness because we do not have more than we do. And when we do this, we may be tempted to charge the Lord with withholding blessing from us.

The apostle Paul lived different parts of his life in both worlds—in abundance and in poverty. In Philippians 4:11–12, he shared with the church,

> *Not that I speak from want [need], for I
> have learned to be content in whatever
> circumstances I am. I know how to get along
> with humble means, and I also know how to live
> in prosperity; in any and every circumstance*

*I have learned the secret of being filled and
going hungry, both of having abundance and
suffering need.*

What was his secret? It was his complete reliance on and
satisfaction in the Lord—"I can do all things through Him
who strengthens me" (v. 13).

What is contentment? In his book *The Rare Jewel of
Christian Contentment*, Puritan pastor Jeremiah Burroughs
defines it as "that sweet, inward, quiet, gracious frame of
spirit, which freely submits to and delights in God's wise
and fatherly disposal in every condition."[4] How's that for
a bumper sticker! But the thrust of Burroughs' argument
throughout his book is built on the exaltation and satisfaction in God and diminishing the value of ourselves and our
circumstances. It's all about perspective. At one point, he
asserts, "A discontented heart is troubled because he has no
more comfort, but a self-denying man rather wonders that
he has as much as he has."[5]

This leads us to consider a helpful tool that we may use to
learn contentment—to be thankful for all that we *do* have
instead of grumbling over what we *don't* have. Beyond our
basic needs, we can be thankful for our jobs that afford us
the ability to pay our bills. We can be thankful for vehicles
and homes and hobbies and vacations—all the extra things
of life that God gives us beyond our basic needs. Consider
sitting down and writing out a list of everything that God
has given you and thank Him for it. We see an example of
this in the testimony of Jacob who declared to the Lord,

"I am unworthy of all the lovingkindness and of all the faithfulness which You have shown to Your servant; for with my staff only I crossed this Jordan, and now I have become two companies" (Gen. 32:10). Jacob praised God joyfully, acknowledging his utter indebtedness to Him for all that he had received.

Among modern threats to a Christian's contentment and thankfulness, one has come through a popular movement often known as the "health, wealth, and prosperity gospel," or simply "the prosperity gospel." Costi Hinn, a former proponent of the prosperity gospel, defines it as "believing in Jesus leading you to being healthy, wealthy and happy."[6] This view sets itself over and against the divine purposes of God. In essence, Hinn writes, "the prosperity gospel takes the sovereignty of God and tosses it aside, claiming that we can control the God of the universe."[7] By exercising faith, it is believed that we can bend God's will to make us wealthy, prosperous, and successful in this life.

However, the teachings of this movement present a direct affront to the goodness and kindness of God. The prosperity gospel teaches that God is obligated to bless, which would enslave His own will to our will. This is a blasphemous notion. Instead, we understand that God gives to His people out of the goodness and lovingkindness of His heart according to His providential purposes. He owes us nothing! And whatever He gives to us is pure kindness.

PROVIDENTIAL PROVISIONS

Much of what God gives to us materially comes in what we could consider to be "natural" means. But the Lord also blesses His people through other means, even *supernatural* means—in ways that we cannot explain or understand through our normal experiences. There are some that equate the supernatural or miraculous with something spectacular (signs in the sky, resurrections, heavenly encounters, etc.), but God frequently works through *providence*—"the act of purposefully providing for, or sustaining and governing, the world."[8] Through His acts of providence, God brings about, by any means He sees fit, His own desired ends.

We see various examples of this in Scripture. When Joseph was sold into slavery to the Egyptians, it appeared that he had met a grim fate. And yet, through God's providential purposes, Joseph ended up as a servant in Potiphar's house. Despite being wrongfully accused by Potiphar's wife for sexual assault and jailed, Scripture notes, "But the LORD was with Joseph *and extended kindness to him*, and gave him favor in the sight of the chief jailer" (Gen. 39:21, emphasis added). It was this distinct favor that eventually led to Joseph being given the ability to interpret the dream of Pharaoh, which eventually led to his release and appointment to the prime minister of Egypt under Pharaoh. Joseph affirmed this in Genesis 50:20 when he declared to his brothers, "As for you, you meant evil against me, but God meant it for good." The Lord extended kindness through His own providence in ordering events.

We see another example of this in the life of the Israelite priest Ezra. The Lord moved in the heart of the Persian king Artaxerxes to allow the Israelites to return to Jerusalem after their captivity in Babylon. Scripture declares, "The king's heart is like channels of water in the hand of the LORD; He turns it wherever He wishes" (Prov. 21:1). God determines to bend and flex the will of even the mightiest kings to serve His purposes. And it is in this occurrence that Ezra recognized the hand of God and praised Him:

> Blessed be the LORD, the God of our fathers, who has put such a thing as this in the king's heart, to adorn the house of the LORD which is in Jerusalem, and has extended lovingkindness to me *before the king and his counselors and before all the king's mighty princes. Thus I was strengthened according to the hand of the LORD my God upon me, and I gathered leading men from Israel to go up with me.* (Ezra 7:27–28, emphasis added)

No matter the circumstance, God determines to carry out His own purposes, whether through natural or supernatural, miraculous or providential means.

There are other ways that God blesses His people through supernatural, provident means. Beyond orchestrating events, the Lord also accomplishes great acts, not limited to our own personal healing. In the Gospels we find frequent occurrences of Jesus providing physical healing for the people around Him. Yet in many places, we read of His heartfelt motive behind the acts—His own compassion.

Matthew 9:35–36 notes Jesus' journeys through many of the Galilean cities and villages. As He traveled, not only did He teach and proclaim the gospel, but He also healed "every kind of disease and every kind of sickness." But then we read of His motivation: "Seeing the people, He felt compassion for them, because they were distressed and dispirited like sheep without a shepherd" (v. 36). It was His compassion— His inward feelings of lovingkindness toward them—that motivated His miraculous healing ministry (cf. Matt. 14:14; 15:32; Mark 6:34). When two men fell down at His feet, begging to be healed of their blindness, Matthew 20:34 records, "Moved with compassion, Jesus touched their eyes; and immediately they regained their sight and followed Him." When a weeping mother who had lost her only son passed by Him, Luke 7:13 notes, "When the Lord saw her, He felt compassion for her, and said to her, 'Do not weep.'" Immediately He touched the coffin and raised the young man from the dead. These kinds of occurrences were a part of Jesus' regular earthly ministry.

What about today? Does God still heal people? In His great wisdom, God designed our bodies with an immune system, which aids us in fighting off sickness and disease. Any time we recover from an illness, we ought to give glory to God. But God also provides doctors and physicians who can treat us. He also provides remedies and medicines. And while we know that a doctor cannot technically "heal" a person themselves, we always pray for them to exercise wisdom and skill to know how to treat us.

In fact, it is not uncommon for some new innovative medical treatment to be called a "miracle cure" because we understand that our bodies need treatment that exists outside ourselves in order to be made well. And when those treatments are so remarkable, we think of them working "miraculously." But there's another way that God heals.

There are times when a sick person is healed not through normal or natural means (i.e., their immune system, doctor-prescribed treatments), but through an act of God; a divine miracle. When a person is sick one moment and then, in the next moment, they are made well by the power of God, we understand that it is because He is working through super-natural means.

The debate rages today regarding the nature of divine healing in this age. While I do not have the space to exhaust all aspects of it here, it is important to note that God reserves the right to do whatever He wants to do, whenever He wants to do it. This includes divine healing. The modern prosperity gospel movement wrongly tricks people into believing that, with enough faith, with enough money, *and through the right "anointed" person*, they can receive physical healing. Not only is this a terrible abuse of the poor and afflicted; there is not a single verse in Scripture that supports this. We cannot demand, buy, or extract blessings from God.

However, God reserves the right to bless people in any way He chooses. If the Lord heals you of a sickness or affliction, praise Him! Give God all glory and honor for His works. Whether God heals a migraine headache or life-threatening cancer, such a blessing is granted freely by God as a demonstration of His kindness. But what if God chooses not to bless or heal? What if we are left to our own pain and afflictions?

That's what we will discuss in the next chapter.

Chapter Six

GOD'S KINDNESS IN SUFFERING

For if He causes grief, then He will have compassion according to His abundant lovingkindness. **(Lam. 3:32)**

When we think about God's kindness to us, we don't tend to include our trials, afflictions, and suffering. We categorize them as something else, perhaps punishment for something we have done wrong, or maybe even some sort of evil that falls outside of the Lord's sovereign control. However, the Bible does not teach that at all. Instead, we read the testimony of Paul, "And we know that God causes all things to work together for good to those who love God, to those who are called according to His purpose" (Rom. 8:28). Certainly, we would regard *good things* as part of the "all things" mentioned in the verse. But what about *bad things*? What about trials, afflictions, pain, and suffering? As we will see, not only are they to be included as part of "all things" working together for good, but they are in fact demonstrations of God's kindness to us.

THE MAN WHO REFUSED TO CURSE GOD

The Old Testament records the story of a man named Job who "was blameless, upright, fearing God and turning away from evil" (Job 1:1). He was blessed with a large family, as well as much prosperity. Scripture notes that "that man was the greatest of all the men of the east" (v. 3). Moreover, he led his family spiritually, offering sacrifices to the Lord on behalf of his children (v. 5). In short, Job was a godly man.

One day Satan, who "prowls around like a roaring lion, seeking someone to devour" (1 Peter 5:8), approached the throne of God. Almost unbelievably, the Lord asked Satan, "Have you considered My servant Job? For there is no one like him on the earth, a blameless and upright man, fearing God and turning away from evil" (Job 1:8). In posing this question, God offered Job to Satan as an example of faith, which would ultimately result in Job's affliction. However, the devil pushed back. After all, Satan reasoned, Job only feared the Lord because he had such a good life. "But put forth Your hand now and touch all that he has; he will surely curse You to Your face," Satan argued (v. 11). God responded by giving Satan permission to afflict Job but within certain boundaries—he could not harm Job himself.

Immediately Satan fled God's presence and descended on Job's livelihood to destroy it. In four concussive acts, one right after another, Satan obliterated Job's wealth by bringing destruction on his livestock (vv. 13–15), his flocks (v. 16), and his camels (v. 17), as well as all the servants who were stewarding Job's possessions. Within moments, Job learned that the bulk of his earthly possessions had been taken from him. But then, he received the worst news yet—all of his children had died tragically when a house collapsed on them (v. 19). Now Job had lost everything.

At hearing the news at losing everything he held dear, the Bible records that "Job arose and tore his robe and shaved his head"—all signs of severe mourning—"and he fell to the ground and worshiped" (v. 20). Worshiped? After losing all his wealth and his family? But remember, Job was a God-fearing man. He said, "Naked I came from my mother's womb, and naked I shall return there. The LORD gave and the LORD has taken away. Blessed be the name of the LORD" (v. 21).

And then comes the most shocking revelation: "Through all this Job did not sin nor did he blame God" (v. 22). But Satan was not done.

In Job 2 we read that Satan approached the throne of God a second time, and *for a second time*, the Lord presented Job as an example of faithfulness, to which Satan scoffed. He complained that the horrendous trial was ineffective because God did not allow him to afflict Job's body. However, he reasoned, "put forth Your hand now, and touch his bone and his flesh; he will curse You to Your face" (2:5). Now, Satan was seeking permission to unleash hell on Job's own person. Again God gave Satan permission to afflict Job but again with parameters—he could not kill him. And again, Satan agreed.

In the very next scene, Satan unleashed painful boils "from the sole of his foot to the crown of his head" (v. 7). This drove Job to the brink of absolute misery. The text tells us that he sat down in ashes, scraping the skin off his body with a piece of broken pottery. As if to pour salt on his wounds, his wife taunted him, saying, "Do you still hold fast your integrity? Curse God and die!" (v. 9). Now even his wife had forsaken him. Job had nothing.

However, he did not listen to the wickedness of his wife. In verse 10 he responded to her, "You speak as one of the foolish women speaks. Shall we indeed accept good from God and not accept adversity?" Despite losing everything—his wealth, his children, his health, and his wife (to desertion), Job never once attacked the character of God or questioned His goodness. "In all this Job did not sin with his lips" (v. 10). In many cases, a person who has experienced the severity of Job's suffering would have rejected the notion of God's kindness. But not Job. What did he understand that many do not? While the next thirty chapters of the book of Job record his misery, laments, and dialogues with others, he never turned his back on God.

Job's plight raises a tough question. Does God still demonstrate His kindness to His people in the midst of trials and suffering? Furthermore, how exactly do afflictions and suffering work together for good (Rom. 8:28)?

HOW GOD DEMONSTRATES HIS KINDNESS THROUGH AFFLICTIONS

Why does God cause families to experience bankruptcy, or parents to lose children, or a mother of five to endure breast cancer? Over the years, many students of Scripture have observed various uses for trials and suffering within the purposes of God. However, for our exploration I have noted the following twelve reasons God demonstrates His kindness through trials, afflictions, and suffering.

First, suffering *proves that we belong to God.* Both times when the Lord offered up Job to Satan to be afflicted, He declared of him, "For there is no one like him on the earth, a blameless and upright man, fearing God and turning away from evil" (Job 1:8; cf. 2:3). In this statement, God was presenting Job to the devil as an example of a true believer. However, both times Satan rejected the Lord's statement, claiming that Job only *appeared* to be genuine because God had blessed him. And so, to prove the genuineness and validity of Job's faith in God, he was put to the test. In the final analysis, Job repented of his grumbling against the Lord and reaffirmed His faith in the sovereignty and goodness of God (Job 42:1–6), thus thwarting Satan's attempts to undermine God's glory.

In 1 Peter 1:6–7, we see this truth illustrated powerfully. We read, "In this you greatly rejoice, even though now for a little while, if necessary, you have been distressed by various trials, so that *the proof of your faith*, being more precious than gold which is perishable, even though tested by fire, may be found to result in praise and glory and honor at the revelation of Jesus Christ" (emphasis added). Despite their experiencing the distressing weight of trials, Peter encouraged believers to "greatly rejoice," even to "praise and glory" in the Lord. Why? Because our faith is being proved through fiery trials.

Much like with the affliction of Job, suffering proves both to Satan and to ourselves that we belong to God. Because when the trial comes to an end, we arrive at the other side praising God rather than cursing Him. When our faith survives—though all else may be lost—it proves beyond the shadow of a doubt that we are His. As Thomas Boston writes, "If one can stand that test, he is manifested to be a saint, a sincere servant of God, as Job was proved to be; if not, he is but a hypocrite: he cannot stand the test . . . but goes away like dross in God's furnace."[1] When we understand that our trials and suffering are proof that we are God's own beloved children, we quickly see that the act of proving our adoption is a tremendous kindness to us.

Suffering also *reveals our weaknesses and sins*. When trials assail us, our natural defenses fall. Any attempt at self-righteousness or good works utterly fails and we are left with the shattered vessel that is underneath. Scripture repeatedly likens suffering to a refiner's fire. Like a refiner's fire, suffering has productive purposes. When considering the sinfulness of the people of Israel, the Lord promised, "I will . . . smelt away your dross as with lye and will remove your alloy" (Isa. 1:25). The imagery pictured here is of a metallurgist heating up a piece of steel until it's glowing orange, and then beating and scraping all the impurities out of it until it becomes pure.

When Job considered the afflictions he had received, while he did not understand their purpose, he knew that "when [the Lord] has tried me, I shall come forth as gold"

(Job 23:10). When the Lord had afflicted Israel, He declared, "Behold, I have refined you, but not as silver; I have tested you in the furnace of affliction" (Isa. 48:10). While the imagery is vivid, it is consistently clear that "the refining pot is for silver and the furnace for gold, but the LORD tests hearts" (Prov. 17:3). Suffering is the furnace, the dross is weaknesses and sins of the heart, and the Lord God is the Refiner who labors with the metal until it has been made pure (cf. Ps. 66:10).

Why does the Lord refine our hearts with such intense fire? It is because of His great lovingkindness that He does not give us over to our own sins, or let us wither away in our polluted condition. He purges us, exposing our sins, and reveals our spiritual deformities, in order that we can repent to the Lord and seek restoration in Him. The only way we will ever grow is if the Lord reveals the dross within our hearts. Suffering is the Lord's way of purifying His people.

We also see that suffering *dislodges our hearts from the world.* The Bible tells us not to love the world—the earthly kingdom of darkness set up against the righteous ways of the Lord. "For all that is in the world," John wrote, "the lust of the flesh and the lust of the eyes and the boastful pride of life, is not from the Father, but is from the world" (1 John 2:16). When we are redeemed by Jesus Christ out of that darkness (Col. 1:13) into God's kingdom of righteousness and light, our hearts still must be dislodged from our old way of living. How does the Lord remove us from the world while we are still living in it? Through suffering and trials.

In his timeless classic *Confessions*, fifth-century pastor and theologian Augustine of Hippo recounts his spiritual journey from being a lover of the things of the world to a lover of the things of God. He confesses to the Lord his former desires, which existed as lusts within him, but then praises God for prying him away from the deadly grip of the world:

> I was eager for fame and wealth and marriage, but you only derided these ambitions. They caused me to suffer the most galling difficulties, but the less you allowed me to find pleasure in anything that was not yourself, the greater, I know, was your goodness to me. Look into my heart, O Lord, for it was your will that I should remember these things and confess them to you. I pray now that my soul may cling to you, for it was you who released it from the deadly snare in which it was so firmly caught.[2]

Our addiction to worldly things often dies hard. And almost always, the only way to sever the "old self, which is being corrupted in accordance with the lusts of deceit" (Eph. 4:22) is to suffer hardship under the hand of God. In the throes of suffering, our hearts do not cling to the fleeting pleasures of earthly things, but to the God who delivers us out of spiritual deadness and into new life. Worldliness is a deadly spiritual addiction. But in God's kindness, He detoxifies us through trials and suffering.

Not only that, but suffering also *disciplines us as beloved children*. When we are born again in Christ Jesus, the Bible teaches that we are not just saved, but adopted as beloved children (e.g., Rom. 8:15–17). One of the ways that we know experientially that we are God's children is that He disciplines us as our Father. Hebrews 12:7 teaches, "God deals with you as with sons; for what son is there whom his father does not discipline?" The writer of Hebrews reasoned that if we do *not* receive any kind of discipline from our heavenly Father, we are to be regarded as illegitimate children (v. 8).

And so, we are reminded by Proverbs 3:11, "My son, do not reject the discipline of the LORD, or loathe His reproof." In fact, the Lord disciplines those whom He loves. But why must our Father discipline us? Because we are sinful. And to leave us in our sins and allow us to live the rest of our lives wallowing in the cancerous sins of our own demise would utterly destroy us. Therefore, "He disciplines us for our good, so that we may share His holiness" (Heb. 12:10). Furthermore, we are assured, "All discipline for the moment seems not to be joyful, but sorrowful; yet to those who have been trained by it, afterwards it yields the peaceful fruit of righteousness" (v. 11). In the same way a loving earthly father disciplines his own children for their good, our perfect heavenly Father demonstrates His lovingkindness to us through our discipline.

In addition, suffering *humbles us*. While the Lord is opposed to all sins, Scripture seems to elevate the sin of pride above all the rest (Prov. 6:17). A person guilty of pride seeks to exalt themselves while at the same time diminishing others. Yet the epitome of pride is when a fallen, sinful person dares to think that they belong in God's place of honor, or even higher. In the face of such a detestable sin, the Bible teaches that "God is opposed to the proud, but gives grace to the humble" (James 4:6; cf. 1 Peter 5:5). The Lord hates pride and has promised to destroy the haughty (Prov. 16:5). But for those who have been humbled, He is gracious and kind.

But how, then, is a proud person to be made humble? Perhaps the most effective way of humbling a person is through trials. The apostle Paul testified that, despite the privileges he experienced in beholding heavenly revelations, the Lord afflicted him with "a thorn in the flesh" to keep him from exalting himself (2 Cor. 12:7). While we do not know what this thorn was—he refers to it as "a messenger of Satan"—the affliction served its purpose of weakening Paul to the point of relying on God alone (v. 9–10). The result of Paul's suffering was contentment with God's sovereign purposes.

This is what suffering does; it humbles us under the mighty hand of God. After all, it's hard to be puffed up while laid up in a hospital bed or standing in line at the food bank. However, Proverbs 16:19 instructs us that "it is better to be humble in spirit with the lowly than to divide the spoil with the proud." And if God opposes the proud, then the kindest thing He could do for us is to humble us by any means necessary so that we might become recipients of His grace.

As another benefit, suffering *realigns our focus on God and brings us closer to Him.* When things seem to be going well in our life, we tend not to lean on the Lord as much. Our spiritual disciplines grow slack. Our prayer life becomes weak and lifeless. Our mind wanders away from thinking about God in favor of making our own plans for the future. In short, in good seasons, we wander away from God.

However, suffering has a way of drawing us back to the Lord. The writer of Psalm 119 echoed this sentiment: "Before I was afflicted I went astray, but now I keep Your word" (Ps. 119:67). When we're hurting, we do not look for outside assistance because we inherently know that only God is able to help us. In this way, our mind quickly shifts back toward the Lord. We pray more. We read the Scriptures more, especially the Psalms. We wait more on the Lord for His sustaining grace. And in this way, our communion with Him grows deeper and richer. We hear this testimony from David in Psalm 63:6–8,

> *When I remember You on my bed,*
> *I meditate on You in the night watches,*
> *For You have been my help,*
> *and in the shadow of Your wings I sing for joy.*
> *My soul clings to You;*
> *Your right hand upholds me.*

After enduring trials, the psalmist concludes, "It is good for me that I was afflicted, that I may learn Your statutes" (Ps. 119:71). Furthermore, he credits God's own faithfulness as the reason for his affliction, as the act of drawing him back to the Lord demonstrates His lovingkindness (v. 75).

As our focus aligns more closely with God, we also find

that He draws near to us and is with us in the midst of our suffering. Not only will He never leave us nor forsake us (Deut. 31:8), but in some ways we might become more acutely aware of the kindness of His presence as we walk through the trials.

What's more, suffering *tests our faith and makes it stronger.* One of the greatest purposes of trials and suffering is to test the strength of our faith. More than simply proving the *existence* of saving faith, affliction proves the *durability* of our faith. This is because we are not only *saved* by faith in Christ, but we are *sustained* daily by our faith in Christ (Gal. 3:3–5). And trials are the means by which our continuous faith is tested and grown by the Lord.

We read in James 1:2–4, "Consider it all joy, my brethren, when you encounter various trials, knowing that the testing of your faith produces endurance. And let endurance have its perfect result, so that you may be perfect and complete, lacking in nothing." There is a direct correlation between difficult trials and the maturing of faith. The more our faith in God is put to the test, the stronger it grows. It becomes more durable and able to withstand a greater amount of affliction. On the contrary, a faith that has not been tested will crumble at the first sign of trouble.

However, God desires that our faith endure for our whole lifetime as a Christian. Romans 5:3–4 encourages us to "exult [rejoice; gloriously exclaim] in our tribulations, knowing that tribulation brings about perseverance; and perseverance, proven character; and proven character, hope."

How does our hope grow as a result of tribulation and suffering? Because in the consistent maturing of our Christian character, we see evidence that "the love of God has been poured out within our hearts through the Holy Spirit who was given to us" (v. 5). God grows us because He loves us.

Suffering also *makes us spiritually indestructible.* As our faith continues to grow in the fires of adversity, it becomes battle-tested, especially if it has endured a diversity of trials. After decades of trials, a Christian becomes trained to turn to God at the first signs of affliction. Our knee-jerk reaction is no longer to fall apart in doubt and worry, but to affix our eyes on the Lord, who has proven faithful time and time again. In this way, suffering has produced an indestructible armor for us. This is why Ephesians 6:16 likens our faith to a shield that is "able to extinguish all the flaming arrows of the evil one." As the years pass, suffering tends not to faze us as much, and nothing surprises us anymore.

Not only does suffering create spiritual armor for us, but it also functions as an offensive weapon. We read in 1 Peter 4:1–2, "Therefore, since Christ has suffered in the flesh, arm yourselves also with the same purpose, because he who has suffered in the flesh has ceased from sin, so as to live the rest of the time in the flesh no longer for the lusts of men, but for the will of God." More than simply enduring pain and suffering, we are instructed to *arm ourselves* with suffering. Why? Because when we come under fire, our battle-tested faith will wage war against our sinful impulses and steel itself toward obedience to the will of God. In this way, suffering actually accelerates a Christian into spiritual maturity. And when a seasoned believer completes the race at the end of their life, their faith in Christ will have been perfected through a lifetime of suffering.

Continuing the progression, suffering *conforms us to the image of Christ.* In his letter to the dispersed churches, Peter informed believers that they had actually been "called for [the] purpose" of suffering (1 Peter 2:21). However, it is not a self-destructive, ascetic kind of suffering, but an identification with the One who suffered for us—the Lord Jesus Christ. Peter elaborates that "Christ also suffered for you, leaving you an example for you to follow in His steps." Our Lord suffered on the cross and "bore our sins in His body" (v. 24) in order to take away God's punishment meant for us. However, as we live our lives, we are meant to look upon His suffering and "die to sin and live to righteousness" (v. 24). In this way, a life of suffering and self-denial becomes instructive for us.

There is more than this, however. When we identify with Christ's suffering, we are submitting to our union with Him. Jesus told His disciples, "If they persecuted Me, they will also persecute you" (John 15:20). In this way, suffering for the cause of Christ is an evidence that we belong to Him. This is what compelled Paul to affirm, "Now I rejoice in my sufferings for your sake, and in my flesh I do my share on behalf of His body, which is the church, in filling up what is lacking in Christ's afflictions" (Col. 1:24). This is not to say that Christ's sufferings were insufficient; rather Paul is identifying His own unique sufferings as belonging to the cause of Christ. In other words, whatever affliction Paul experienced because of Christ was ultimately meant to be cast upon the Lord by those who hate Him.

But as we imitate Jesus Christ in His life, we also are meant to imitate Him in His sufferings and death; and in our identification with Him in these things, we also share with Him in His glorious resurrection and ascension to the heavenly places (Eph. 2:6). Our union with Jesus Christ is so strong and so secure, it led Paul to declare: "I have been crucified with Christ; and it is no longer I who live, but Christ lives in me; and the life which I now live in the flesh I live by faith in the Son of God, who loved me and gave Himself up for me" (Gal. 2:20). God desires that we be conformed to the image of Christ (Rom. 8:29; cf. Phil. 3:10). And the more we are conformed to His image—in life, in thought, in speech, in conduct, in suffering, and in death—the more we see that it is perhaps one of the greatest kindnesses of God to us that we should become like His own beloved Son.

Suffering also *deepens our love for other Christians.* Trials and suffering do not just work for our own benefit. In addition to experiencing "the fellowship of [Christ's] sufferings" (Phil. 3:10), there is also another fellowship of suffering—with other believers. Not only is there a fellowship of common experience among believers who suffer together, but there is also a charge for us to help one another in our affliction. As we endure hardship and receive comfort from God, we are meant to extend that same comfort to others.

Second Corinthians 1 begins with an exhortation of

such comfort. We are told that God "comforts us in all our affliction *so that* we will be able to comfort those who are in any affliction with the comfort with which we ourselves are comforted by God" (v. 4, emphasis added). For example, when a woman has survived breast cancer by the grace of God, she may be far better equipped to encourage another woman who receives her first diagnosis. In this way, we are able to be both "sharers of our sufferings" as well as "sharers of our comfort" (v. 7).

The more we are afflicted with trials and suffering, the more equipped we become to help others who are in pain. And as we consider those around us, we are able to "love one another" (John 13:34) in very tangible ways—through tenderness, service, prayer, compassion, empathy, and biblical counsel. We would also do well to consider that perhaps our own particular trials have been given to us so that, once we have endured faithfully through them, we may be able to help someone else who is suffering in the same way. And in doing so, not only are our hearts knit to them, but theirs to us. As the bond of loving unity grows between believers, we see the kindness of God to grow this sweet fellowship in His grace.

As our eleventh observation, suffering *bears witness to the power of the gospel.* One of the most unexpected results of suffering is its effectiveness in bearing witness to the gospel of Jesus Christ. When the apostles were arrested and jailed for preaching the gospel in Acts 5, the religious leaders of Israel had no idea that their persecution would serve to grow the church in Jerusalem. Before being released, the disciples were whipped and implored to remain silent, yet the men returned to the streets, "rejoicing that they had been considered worthy to suffer shame for His name. And every day . . . they kept right on teaching and preaching Jesus as the Christ" (Acts 5:41–42). What was the result of their labors? Acts 6:1 tells us that the number of disciples continued to increase.

The key to this remarkable growth is the evangelistic boldness that comes from those who suffer in bearing witness to Christ. While in prison, Paul testified, "my circumstances have turned out for the greater progress of the gospel . . . and that most of the brethren, trusting in the Lord because of my imprisonment, have far more courage to speak the word of God without fear" (Phil. 1:12, 14). How so?

Oftentimes, the fear of persecution stifles us from being faithful to the gospel. We keep quiet when we ought to be sharing Christ with others. But when we see how God faithfully sustains His servants in the height of their afflictions, we are emboldened to stand for Christ, knowing that He will sustain our faith in the same way. When we consider that through evangelism the gospel of God is unleashed to save the lost (cf. Rom. 1:16), then whatever means by which the message goes forth—including through persecution and suffering—is a demonstration of the lovingkindness of God toward sinners.

Finally, suffering *displays God's power and glory.* Many times it feels like we are suffering for no reason at all. There is no purpose, or so we think. When Jesus passed by a blind man in John 9, the disciples stopped and asked Him,

"Rabbi, who sinned, this man or his parents, that he would be born blind?" This was a sound theological question, as it would have been natural to assume in their culture that physical sickness was the result of sinfulness. However, Jesus surprised them by answering, "It was neither that this man sinned, nor his parents; but it was so that the works of God might be displayed in him" (v. 3). Immediately, Jesus ministered to the man, applied mud to his eyes, and sent him to the pool of Siloam to wash himself. When the man returned, his eyes were healed!

Over and over again in Scripture, we see that even in adversity and affliction, God is glorified. When God took away the strength of Gideon's army, dwindling it down to three hundred soldiers, He told Gideon, "The people who are with you are too many for Me to give Midian into their hands, for Israel would become boastful, saying, 'My own power has delivered me'" (Judg. 7:2). For Gideon, the shrinking of his army from thirty-two thousand down to three hundred posed a substantial threat to him. Humanly speaking, they surely would have died. But God used this trial of faith to glorify Himself so that, when the army was victorious, it would be unquestionable whose hand had delivered them.

When we suffer in our affliction and God sustains or delivers us, it serves to demonstrate to us and others that it is *His* power at work, and not ours. This is why Paul boasted in the Lord despite his own debilitating trials: "Most gladly, therefore, I will rather boast about my weaknesses, so that the power of Christ may dwell in me" (2 Cor. 12:9). Suffering puts the power and glory of God on display. This is why Peter declared that "if anyone suffers as a Christian, he is not to be ashamed, but is to glorify God in this name" (1 Peter 4:16). In God's kindness, He permits us to behold His power and glory in the face of our afflictions.

GOD'S PURPOSES ABOVE OUR PAIN

After receiving bad counsel from his three friends, Job finally received good counsel from a young man named Elihu. Whereas Job's other friends had foolishly tried to blame Job's misfortunes on some sort of wrongdoing, Elihu administered godly counsel. In the end, Job's sufferings did not exist apart from the sovereign hand of God. Elihu observed, "Whether for correction, or for His world, *or for lovingkindness*, He causes it to happen" (Job 37:13, emphasis added). We may never know the full reasons for our suffering, but we can trust that God has His own providential purposes. The Lord declares, "For as the heavens are higher than the earth, so are My ways higher than your ways and My thoughts than your thoughts" (Isa. 55:9).

And while we may never understand why bad things happen to us, or all of what God intends to teach us, we can be assured, "the Lord's lovingkindnesses indeed never cease, for His compassions never fail. They are new every morning; great is Your faithfulness" (Lam. 3:22–23). Furthermore, "if He causes grief, then He will have compassion according to His abundant lovingkindness" (v. 32).

Chapter Seven

GOD'S KINDNESS REFLECTED IN THE BELIEVER

Be kind to one another, tender-hearted,
forgiving each other, just as God in Christ
also has forgiven you. **(Eph. 4:32)**

Had he killed Mephibosheth, David would have been within his rights as king. After all, he was the son of Jonathan, grandson of Saul—David's archenemy. Being a descendent of the house of Saul, he could have been viewed as a threat to David's reign. But David did not see it this way.

In 2 Samuel 9, David defied all perceivable logic and asked, "Is there not yet anyone of the house of Saul to whom I may show the kindness of God?" (v. 3). Then he was told of Jonathan's surviving son, Mephibosheth, who had been severely crippled in both of his feet because of a terrible accident when he was five years old. David sent for him, and when he arrived, he came and fell on his face before the king, no doubt scared of what might happen to him. However, David spoke gently to him, saying, "Do not fear, for I will surely show kindness to you for the sake of your father Jonathan, and will restore to you all the land of your grandfather Saul; and you shall eat at my table regularly" (v. 7).

We then read that David blessed Mephibosheth by restoring to him all of Saul's wealth, as well as his land. With Saul dead and gone, David could have seized it all for himself, but he generously gave it to the young man who would otherwise have nothing. At first, Mephibosheth had regarded himself as nothing more than "a dead dog" (v. 8), but David treated him as an honored guest, even family. In the final verse of the account, we read: "So Mephibosheth lived in Jerusalem, for he ate at the king's table regularly. Now he was lame in both feet" (v. 13). What a remarkable picture of the kindness of the king!

But what was David's motivation for his actions? It no doubt stemmed in part from David's deep affection for his friend Jonathan—whom "he loved as himself" (1 Sam. 18:1, 3)—and from David's realization that he himself was a debtor to God's grace, and a recipient of the Lord's lovingkindness.

THE MOTIVATIONS AND PRACTICES OF KINDNESS

When we consider the plentiful expressions of God's kindness displayed throughout Scripture, it is hard not to be overwhelmed with gratitude. Beyond this, beholding the kindness of God motivates us to imitate His example. In fact, the *only* appropriate active response to receiving kindness is to show kindness to others.

Scripture's persistent refrain is that we would be obedient to God's commands to be kind. Solomon writes, "Do not let kindness and truth leave you; bind them around your neck, write them on the tablet of your heart" (Prov. 3:3; cf. 14:22; 19:22; 31:26). We read in Micah 6:8, "He has told you, O man, what is good; and what does the LORD require of you but to do justice, *to love kindness*, and to walk humbly with your God?" (emphasis added). All throughout the New Testament, we see kindness listed as a Christian virtue (e.g., 2 Cor. 6:6; Gal. 5:22; Col. 3:12; 2 Peter 1:7). In fact, we read that "Love . . . is kind" (1 Cor. 13:4). The command is inescapable.

But it's more than a general maxim. It's not simply that we are to value kindness as some sort of obscure virtue. Rather we are commanded to practice kindness regularly, making it a part of our daily lives. Peter exhorted Christians to "be harmonious, sympathetic, brotherly, *kindhearted*, and humble in spirit; not returning evil for evil or insult for insult but giving a blessing instead; for you were called for the very purpose that you might inherit a blessing" (1 Peter 3:8–9, emphasis added). Here he provided several examples of what kindness looks like, including harmonious living, sympathy toward others, friendliness, humility, kind words and actions, even giving material blessings to others.

Such actions are more than simply altruistic efforts. This

isn't just kindness for kindness's sake. Christians are meant to manifest kindness to others in an effort to foster true unity within the body of Christ. As Paul commanded, we are to be "diligent to preserve the unity of the Spirit in the bond of peace" (Eph. 4:3). He gave several practical behaviors that contribute to this end, but concluded his discourse with a final plea: "Let all bitterness and wrath and anger and clamor and slander be put away from you, along with all malice. *Be kind to one another*, tender-hearted, forgiving each other, just as God in Christ also has forgiven you" (Eph. 4:31–32, emphasis added).

What is groundbreaking about Christian kindness is that it defies the selfish cruelty of the world. Where the world says, "Hold that grudge! Get your pound of flesh! Hit 'em back harder!" the Bible tells us to "be kind to one another, tender-hearted, [and] forgiving . . ." Why? Because the Lord has demonstrated kindness to us through His compassion, forgiveness, and saving grace. Even when we were His enemies, He redeemed and saved us. We owe Him no less than our very lives!

And so, we show kindness out of obedience to the Lord. As we have noted several times throughout this book regarding the Grand Premise: *God is good; we are sinful. Because of this, we are undeserving of His goodness. But because of God's mercy, He demonstrates lovingkindness to us. Therefore every kindness we experience is pure grace and ought to be received with gladness and thankfulness.* And if this premise is true, we ought to be kind to all people (cf. 2 Tim. 2:24), because in demonstrating Christian kindness, we reflect the kindness of God displayed in the gospel of Jesus Christ. We remember that "when the kindness of God our Savior and His love for mankind appeared, He saved us" (Titus 3:4–5). We are called to be kind to others because God has been immeasurably kind to us.

A PORTRAIT OF KINDNESS

But how do we see God-like kindness portrayed by others? We have already looked at David's kindness toward Mephibosheth, the grandson of his enemy. Let us consider another example given to us by the Lord Himself.

In what is known as the parable of the good Samaritan, we find a portrait of kindness in Scripture spoken by Jesus, told through a parable in Luke 10. It comes on the heels of a question posed to Jesus by a lawyer who asked, "Teacher, what shall I do to inherit eternal life?" (v. 25). Jesus responded by asking him if the man had read the Scriptures. "What is written in the Law? How does it read to you?" He asked (v. 26). The man responded by quoting both Deuteronomy 6:5 and Leviticus 19:18, "You shall love the Lord your God with all your heart, and with all your soul, and with all your strength, and with all your mind; and your neighbor as yourself" (Luke 10:27). Concurring with the statement, Jesus replied in verse 28, "You have answered correctly; *do* this and you will live" (emphasis added).

However, Luke records that the inquisitive lawyer is not

genuine in his approach to Jesus. Verse 25 records that in posing the question, the lawyer was seeking "to put [Jesus] to the test." He was not truly seeking to understand the way of salvation. Furthermore, we read in verse 29 that the man was looking "to justify himself" by asking, "And who is my neighbor?" He does not ask this because he truly wants to know. Rather his heart is no doubt puffed up with pride because he believes that he has already fulfilled the requirements, both loving God and his Jewish neighbors. Yet he still asked, "And who is my neighbor?" Jesus' answer would have shocked him and those standing around in the crowd.

Jesus then tells the parable of a man who makes a journey on foot from Jerusalem to Jericho. Along the way, he is attacked by a small band of thieves who strip him of his clothing and possessions, beat him mercilessly, and leave him for dead (v. 30). The man is now in desperate need of help. Who will come to his rescue?

Two men pass by on the road, first a priest, then a Levite. Both men steer clear of the bloody mess of a man, passing him by "on the other side" (vv. 31–32). However, a Samaritan approaches the man, and when he sees him, Jesus notes, "he felt compassion" (v. 33). At this point in the parable, Jesus likely would have seen the eyebrows of His listeners pop up. Jesus continues by noting that the Samaritan "came to him and bandaged up his wounds, pouring oil and wine on them; and he put him on his own beast, and brought him to an inn and took care of him. On the next day he took out two denarii and gave them to the innkeeper and said, 'Take care of him; and whatever more you spend, when I return I will repay you'" (vv. 34–35).

I imagine Jesus would have heard some gasps. Why? Because the Jews regarded the Samaritans with contempt—spiritual half-breeds who were not worth crossing the street to even spit upon. Yet Jesus portrays a Samaritan demonstrating unusual kindness to a stranger, no doubt a Jew.

The extent of the Samaritan's compassion is remarkable. Not only does he bandage up the stranger's wounds and tends to him, but he gently lifts the man onto his own beast of burden. Had he merely bandaged the man up and walked away, he would have already done more for him than the other two men who passed by. But the Samaritan goes ever further and brings the man to an inn to recover. Beyond this, he spares no expense, incurring the full debt of the man's stay without specifying a time frame. What if the man had stayed three days? A week? Two weeks? The Samaritan vows to return and pay the debt. This is profound kindness.

At this point, Jesus turns back to the lawyer in the crowd and asks, "Which of these three do you think proved to be a neighbor to the man who fell into the robbers' hands?" (v. 36). Considering that the lawyer likely felt the same disdain for Samaritans as every other Jew in Israel, it would have pained him to admit, "The one who showed mercy toward him." But clearly it was the right answer; it was the *only* answer! Following the lawyer's answer, Jesus commands him, "Go and do the same" (v. 37).

The parable contains many applicable truths for us.

Within the story we see a demonstration of the quality of kindness that the Lord values—a compassionate, selfless, generous kindness that spares no expense, even toward a complete stranger. One is hard-pressed to find a greater example noted elsewhere in Scripture. However, the most shocking aspect of the account comes when we consider Jesus' audience and their antipathy toward the Samaritan in the parable. Not only does Jesus articulate an example of godly kindness, but He tells of such kindness toward those who would otherwise be enemies.

This is the quality of the Lord's own kindness. Every one of us is like the man on the road who was left for dead. In fact, Scripture records that, prior to salvation, we "were dead in [our] trespasses and sins" (Eph. 2:1). Unable to help ourselves, our eventual death was sure. Yet the Lord came along and rescued us, saving our life and paying our way. However, unlike the Samaritan in the story, He was not our enemy; we were His enemies (Rom. 5:10). He would have been justified to turn up His nose and keep walking, but instead He felt compassion on us and saved us by His own lovingkindness.

And in the same way we have been shown such immeasurable kindness, the Lord bids us to "go and do the same" to others—to love our neighbors. Do we do this simply to justify ourselves? Is it good for goodness' sake? No, we demonstrate the kindness of God to others because He has been so kind to us. We are merely reflecting His kindness through our own lives for the world to see.

OVERWHELMED BY KINDNESS

A few years ago, an older couple in my church named Tom and Wilma experienced a challenging health trial. Over the course of their three-decade marriage, the two were accustomed to Wilma being the one to endure physical challenges —life-threatening pneumonia, four bouts of breast cancer (one of which she was told she would not survive), eight years of chemotherapy, and a few failed knee operations that left her walking with a cane. But this time it was Tom's turn.

When Tom began to experience rapid vision loss in one of his eyes, he scheduled an appointment to see the doctor. An MRI revealed a large, benign tumor behind his right eye that would need to be removed through surgery. However, the tumor had wrapped itself around the optic nerve, as well as the carotid artery, which immediately complicated the matter. Once realizing the surgery would be more than he could handle, the local surgeon referred Tom to the head of neurosurgery and oncology at Mass General in Boston, more than two hours away.

Thankfully, the surgery was successful. Seven pieces of titanium and twenty-seven screws later, Tom's skull was reassembled, and he was sent home to recover. However, he was informed that he was also going to need radiation, which would entail driving down to Boston and back several times a week in the dead of a New England winter. Between Tom's post-surgery incapacitation and Wilma's already frail condition, they knew that the daily two-hundred-mile round trip would be near impossible for them.

One of our church members, a young mom who lived an hour in the opposite direction, heard about the couple's ordeal and got to work straightaway. She set up "Tom's Treatment Taxi"—an online fill-in schedule where volunteer drivers could sign up to bring Tom down and back. Forty-eight hours later, all thirty slots were filled—all but three of them by members of our church! In addition, the couple received gift certificates to help offset other expenses, and the whole church became ignited with fervent prayer.

Day after day, week after week, a different car from "Tom's Treatment Taxi" would pull into the driveway, gently load Tom into their vehicle, and take off for the daylong trek. While on the drive, the saints ministered to Tom, talking and sharing, telling stories, and even singing songs. The final day of "Tom's Treatment Taxi" was filled by the young mom who organized the whole ministry. A few years prior, she too had faced a life-threatening brain tumor and needed to undergo a similar surgery. Even at the very end of it all, she would be able to encourage Tom and share her experiences of pain, struggle, and life after surgery.

At every hospital visit, Tom prayed that the Lord would give him opportunities to share his faith and minister to others around him. While strapped to the table with a device bathing his head with radiation, Tom gave himself to singing hymns. He would also ask the hospital staff how he could pray for them, to their great surprise and delight. Even as he was turning to leave, he was able to encourage a mother of two battling breast cancer; he recounted Wilma's story of surviving breast cancers, sharing the gospel with her.

After his final radiation treatment, the hospital staff encouraged Tom to ring the "good luck" bell. As he prepared to ring it, he told the staff huddled around him that he was ringing the bell in thanksgiving to God for their hard work. Then he told them, "I will ring the bell that you may come to know Jesus." With that, the sound of the bell rang out through the halls.

Through the whole ordeal, Tom and Wilma had been overwhelmed with the goodness and lovingkindness of the Lord. At the end of it all, Tom shared:

> *I am thankful for the tumor, the surgery, and radiation—all of it. God used it to show me that He loves me. God used it to show me His love through His church. I can only think that, while the doctor had my head open on the surgical table, God had my heart open and was pouring in an extra measure of His love, grace, and mercy that I now can pour out on others.*[1]

God lavishes His own lovingkindness on His people that they may respond by demonstrating kindness to others. In this way, we reflect His kindness amid a cruel world.

Chapter Eight

GOD'S KINDNESS TO THE NATIONS

---

*"But love your enemies . . . for He Himself is kind
to ungrateful and evil men"* (Luke 6:35)

One of the greatest conundrums in the Bible is how those who love and honor God seem to have a difficult life while those who hate and despise Him seem to live a life of ease and prosperity. When considering his own tragic life, Job lamented, "Why do the wicked still live, continue on, also become very powerful?" (Job 21:7). While the earth piled over the graves of his own children had barely settled, he reasoned of the wicked, "Their descendants are established with them in their sight, and their offspring before their eyes" (v. 8). With Job's livestock all dead and his wealth destroyed, he failed to fathom how "[the wicked's] houses are safe from fear, and the rod of God is not on them" (v. 9). Job simply could not comprehend it.

In a similar vein, others have pondered and lamented, "Why do the wicked prosper?" The psalmist (perhaps David) cried out to the Lord in Psalm 10, "For the wicked boasts of his heart's desire, and the greedy man curses and spurns the Lord. The wicked, in the haughtiness of his countenance, does not seek Him. All his thoughts were, 'There is no God'" (vv. 3–4). This led him to question the Lord why "his ways prosper at all times; Your judgments are on high, out of his sight; as for all his adversaries, he snorts at them" (v. 5). Why does it seem that the Lord is not destroying the wicked who refuse to acknowledge that He exists?

Even the prophet Jeremiah could not seem to arrive at an answer. He cried to the Lord, "Righteous are You, O Lord, that I would plead my case with You; indeed I would discuss matters of justice with You: Why has the way of the wicked prospered? Why are all those who deal in treachery at ease?" (Jer. 12:1).

Over and over again, we read a similar refrain—the cry of the troubled heart who cannot understand why God allows the wicked to survive, even to thrive. When we consider the theme of this book, we could even frame our question like this: "Why does God show kindness to those who are cruel and wicked?" When we perceive that God blesses the unrighteous with good things, it may appear to us that His character is somehow compromised. But is this the case?

COMMON GRACE

To understand why God shows kindness to the wicked, we need to consider a concept theologians refer to as *common grace.* If we define *grace* as God's unmerited favor, then we might say that *common grace* is the favor of God displayed to all people in general. One theologian defines it as "kindness extended to all persons through God's general providence."[1] Another as "the grace of God by which he gives people innumerable blessings that are not part of salvation."[2] We might even define common grace as "indiscriminate kindness"—the expressed goodness of God to all regardless of their saving relationship to Him. However, is this notion a biblical one?

When we survey various texts in Scripture, we find several expressions of God's common grace to all people. We may consider the first expression of God's common grace through *general blessings.* This is the kindness of God displayed to all people in such a way that enables them to enjoy their lives and behold the loveliness of His creation. Jesus taught His disciples that God "causes His sun to rise on the evil and the good, and sends rain on the righteous and the unrighteous" (Matt. 5:45). Even a wicked man can experience the general kindness of God in watching a sunset or enjoying a good meal. After all, James 1:17 says, "Every good thing given and every perfect gift is from above, coming down from the Father of lights." God offers general blessings out of the goodness of His character. "The LORD is gracious and merciful; slow to anger and great in lovingkindness. The LORD is good to all, and His mercies are over all His works" (Ps. 145:8–9). Even in a sin-drenched world, God still permits unbelievers to experience His kindness.

A second expression of common grace is through the *restraint of evil*. Without God's general goodness and gracious kindness shown to all people, the world would rip itself to shreds in no time at all. Yet God extends His kindness to the world through various means—including the restraining of wicked behavior through the human conscience (Rom. 2:15), the restraining of rebellion in children by their parents (Prov. 13:1–2), and the restraining of evil through governmental authorities by which it maintains social order (Rom. 13:1–5). In a somewhat mysterious passage in the New Testament, we even read about "the lawless one" (perhaps either Satan or the Antichrist) who is currently being restrained in the world by the powerful hand of God (2 Thess. 2:6–7). We must see that it is an immense and necessary kindness of God that evil is restrained in the world so that societies may flourish and life can be preserved.

This leads us to a third expression of common grace in *the conviction of sin that leads to salvation*. This is not to say that God's common grace saves all people, but that through God's indiscriminate kindness many people are afforded opportunities to behold the goodness of God, feel the conviction of their sins, and have the opportunity to hear the gospel of Jesus Christ. In fact, John 16:8–11 specifically notes that the Holy Spirit works to "convict the world concerning sin, and righteousness, and judgment." Yet while He convicts the world of sinfulness, God demonstrates His kindness and mercy to withhold His judgment until all who would come to faith in Jesus Christ have been redeemed (2 Peter 3:9).

And so, we see that God's common grace—His indiscriminate kindness—is not exercised arbitrarily or nonchalantly. God has a specific purpose in demonstrating His goodness and reserves the divine right to exercise kindness to the world He created. However, it will not remain forever. God's common grace has an expiration date.

GOD'S KINDNESS AND SEVERITY

Let's return to our earlier question, "Why do the wicked prosper?" The Lord's exhortation comes to us in several places, perhaps most poignantly in Psalm 37. King David, one who had cried similarly to the Lord, encourages us, "Do not fret because of evildoers, be not envious toward wrongdoers. For they will wither quickly like the grass and fade like the green herb" (vv. 1–2). The believer is encouraged not to worry about it. Why? Because the prosperity of the wicked is only temporary.

However, we are encouraged to "trust in the LORD and do good" (v. 3), "delight [ourselves] in the LORD" (v. 4), and "commit [our] way to the LORD" (v. 5). And with the exhortation comes the promise: "He will bring forth your righteousness as the light and your judgment as the noonday" (v. 6). A few verses later we read, "The wicked plots against the righteous and gnashes at him with his teeth. The Lord laughs at him, for He sees his day is coming" (vv. 12–13). In other words, God will vindicate the deeds of the righteous and judge the wicked accordingly.

The Bible consistently portrays this balance between God's kindness and mercy, and His judgment. One prescient passage that displays them both together comes in Romans 11. The apostle Paul provides exhortation and instruction regarding God's dealings with the nation of Israel. Despite the Lord's repeated calls for the nation to repent and trust in Christ, many have hardened their heart in rebellion (Rom. 11:7, 15, 25).

But Paul offers a promise to the nation regarding the nature of those who are the recipients of the Lord's salvation and those who will be judged. He notes, "Behold then the kindness and severity of God; to those who fell, severity, but to you, God's kindness, if you continue in His kindness; otherwise you also will be cut off" (v. 22). In Paul's framework here, there are really only two options: God's severity or God's kindness.

For all who would reject the gospel of Jesus Christ, God reserves only judgment. The Greek word translated "severity" in verse 22 is *hapotomia*, which literally refers to cutting something off completely. Jesus communicates in like manner in John 15:6, referring to those who do not "abide" in Him, as those who are cut off like a branch. He comments, "If anyone does not abide in Me, he is thrown away as a branch and dries up; and they gather them, and cast them into the fire and they are burned." This is all language of final judgement for unbelievers. Despite being the recipients of God's common grace and indiscriminate kindness, if anyone does not manifest genuine faith in Jesus

Christ, they will ultimately be "cut off" and severed from God's lovingkindness forever.

However, Paul continues, if anyone stands in their faith (Romans 11:20), they will remain with Him—they will "continue in His kindness" (v. 22). God makes no provision for people to reject Him in the end. There are only two choices: believe in the Lord or be cut off forever. Despite demonstrating kindness to the world, the Lord will not endure the rebellion of nations forever. When the nations rage against Him and devise evil plans, the Lord scoffs at them in derision (Ps. 2:1–4). And so, what is God's warning to the nations?

> *Now therefore, O kings, show discernment;*
> *Take warning, O judges of the earth.*
> *Worship the Lord with reverence*
> *And rejoice with trembling.*
> *Do homage to the Son, that He not become*
>   *angry, and you perish in the way,*
> *For His wrath may soon be kindled.*
> *How blessed are all who take refuge in Him!*
> *(Ps. 2:10–12)*

However, not every person openly stands in rebellion against the Lord. Not everyone shakes their fists at Him and curses His name publicly. There are some who fly under the banner of Christianity but hold to beliefs and practices that are contrary to the Bible's teaching. And so, what about those who functionally reject God's kindness yet claim the name of Christ?

TWO POPULAR AFFRONTS TO GOD'S TRUE KINDNESS

Right now, we see two popular movements in the West that have infiltrated Christianity and negatively influenced our perceptions of God and the gospel. While it is important to note that not every individual who may fit the following labels are walking in rebellion to the Lord—in fact, many love Christ dearly and seek to follow Him—many of the beliefs and practices within these movements do not lead believers into "standing by [their] faith" and "continuing in [God's] kindness" (Rom. 11:20, 22).

The first is a progressivist theology that is often likened to "social justice." Admittedly, there is a broad spectrum of adherence to the various principles of social justice.[3] Christians should devote themselves to loving their neighbors, advocating for true fairness and biblical justice, standing against injustice against the unborn, and rejecting bigotry against skin color. This is simply faithfulness to Christian orthodoxy and a reflection of thankfulness to God.

However, we often hear supercharged language and divisive rhetoric geared toward demanding blessings, "fairness," or favor. When trumpeted in Christian circles, it sounds very much like a version of the prosperity gospel—that God has promised His people wealth, status, equity, or power through the gospel of Jesus Christ. But nothing of this aligns with what we have learned about God's kindness toward His people. Kindness is not owed to us, nor can it be demanded; it is given freely according to God's own goodness and in accordance with His own divine prerogatives.

The second popular movement that has negatively influenced Christianity is often swept up under the title of "Christian nationalism." Again, there is a broad spectrum of belief and adherence within this movement often couched in "populism."[4] For Christians who hold to a healthy patriotism, a gratitude to God for experiencing national blessings, or a respect for the governmental principles that correspond with a general Christian morality, there is a likelihood of walking in loving obedience to God.

But when we see Christians who platform political leaders to an almost godlike status, regarding them as earthly messiahs, or demanding rights and freedoms by virtue of the belief that God is supposedly in a specific covenant with a nation, there is grave danger present. God does not owe anything to anyone outside of His intent to give graciously out of His own will. Once again, God does not *owe* His kindness to any nation. Furthermore, there is no salvation to be had in earthly saviors, human ingenuity, or man-made charters. The only salvation available to the people of any nation comes through the gospel of Jesus Christ. It is to this gospel we will again turn.

THE ONLY HOPE OF NATIONS

When we consider the challenges and frustrations that we experience in the world, it's hard not to cry out against them. And when we see the sinfulness, cruelty, and evil running rampant around us, we tend to cry out like David: "For the sake of Your name, O LORD, revive me. In Your righteousness bring my soul out of trouble. And in Your lovingkindness, cut off my enemies and destroy all those who afflict my soul, for I am Your servant" (Ps. 143:11–12).

However, the Lord gives us a different prescription. In Luke 6, Jesus encourages the disciples, who He knows will endure horrendous treatment by the world because of their faith. Despite persecution, Jesus tells them to show visible kindness to their oppressors: "Love your enemies, do good to those who hate you, bless those who curse you, pray for those who mistreat you" (vv. 27–28). Even when they are abused or even robbed, they are to give freely and not retaliate (vv. 29–30). After all, it's one thing to show kindness to other believers, or even friends and family. But what about our enemies?

Jesus repeats His command to "love your enemies and do good" to them. However, in verse 35 He gives a reason. Why should we show kindness to our enemies? Because "[God] Himself is kind to ungrateful and evil men." What a remarkable truth to ponder! Despite all the world's unbelief, disrespect, rebellion, cruelty, wickedness, and hatred, God still demonstrates His kindness to the nations. And so, if God "is kind to ungrateful and evil men," then we should show no less kindness to others as well.

However, the Bible maintains that the Lord is the only hope of the nations. We read the beautiful words of David:

> *Your lovingkindness, O Lord, extends to the heavens,*
> *Your faithfulness reaches to the skies.*

Your righteousness is like the mountains of God;
Your judgments are like a great deep.
O LORD, You preserve man and beast.
How precious is Your lovingkindness, O God!
And the children of men take refuge in the
shadow of Your wings.
They drink their fill of the abundance of Your
house;
And You give them to drink of the river of Your
delights.
For with You is the fountain of life;
In Your light we see light. (Ps. 36:5–9)

Behold the all-sufficiency of God in this psalm. Ponder His goodness to all the peoples of the earth. Marvel at the depths of His lovingkindness! As the psalmist prays for the revival of the nation of Israel, consider the responsibility of every believer to pray:

Restore us, O God of our salvation,
And cause Your indignation toward us to cease.
Will You be angry with us forever?
Will You prolong Your anger to all generations?
Will You not Yourself revive us again,
That Your people may rejoice in You?
Show us Your lovingkindness, O LORD,
And grant us Your salvation. (Ps. 85:4–7)

The greatest single act of lovingkindness toward humanity has been displayed to us in the person and work of Jesus Christ. Despite our fallenness and sinfulness against God, Jesus came to earth as a man—complete divinity wrapped in sinless humanity. He lived a perfect life in full obedience to God, fulfilling a perfect righteousness that we could not obtain. He then gave up His life on the cross, satisfying the wrath of God against us, and earning forgiveness for sinners. His body was buried in the ground, and then He rose again from the grave on the third day, in full vigor of life and victory. And in the wake of His resurrection, He ascended back to heaven to sit at the right hand of the Father on high.

This is the message of the gospel of Jesus Christ, in which we are called to believe and obey. Our hope is not found in social programs or community efforts or humanitarian efforts or governments or kings. Our only hope—the hope of every person and every nation—is in the finished work of Jesus Christ. And it is by Him alone that God offers grace, goodness, love, and kindness to the undeserving.

ALL THINGS FOR GOOD

Walking through the front doors, I was hit with the stale smell of disinfectant, triggering a sense memory of every hospital I had ever visited. After signing in, I made my way through the reception area and started toward Susan's room. Only a few months before, she didn't want to see me, but now she did. Her mother met me at the door. After a few hushed words, I walked in and saw her lying in her bed.

This was the second time I had seen Susan since she came to hospice, and she had already diminished quite a bit in just a week. She had since lost the feeling in her left side and the nurses were trying to make her comfortable. She winced and groaned with pain; it was difficult to watch. When it seemed like she was settled enough, I sat down near her bedside and began to speak to her.

Her eighty-year-old mother, Janet, sat down next to me and filled me in on the latest updates. While not saved until she was seventy-one, Janet immediately began telling her whole family—children, grandchildren, great-grandchildren—about Jesus Christ. After her husband died, she moved to Gilmanton and began attending my church where she soon

THE KINDNESS OF GOD

became a member. Her conversations with Susan about the
Lord through the years yielded nothing. But once Susan got
sick, Janet pressed in with her, trying to lead her to Christ.

During her visits, she brought her Bible and read Scripture, praying openly for Susan. When she needed all-night
care, several women from our church volunteered to help.
Many sent cards; everyone prayed. Susan didn't understand
why people who were strangers to her would care. "They
don't even know me, Mom. Why are they sending me cards?"

Janet would respond, "Because they love you, and they
want to help. Maybe they don't know you, but they know
God." Yet Susan still resisted the Lord.

Often tormented by the guilt of her past sins, Susan
would cry, "God will never forgive me for what I did! I
was so bad." But she still refused to be comforted. Janet
struggled to find the words to say, and when she was able to
offer comfort or encouragement, she worried that it wasn't
enough. And now time was running out.

"Susan, the reason I'm here," I said, "is because I want to
talk to you about the Lord." Knowing that I might only have
her attention for a few minutes, I chose my words carefully. I
shared with her the hope of the gospel, to which she repeated
her fears: "I'm scared that God will never forgive me!" I
responded and told her that not only would God forgive her
for everything she had ever done, but Jesus Christ would
save her and give her eternal life with Him in heaven. "If you
trust in Him, He will save you, and you will have eternal
life." I took her hand and held it gently. Romans 10:9 was on

my mind; I had shared it before: "If you confess with your mouth Jesus as Lord, and believe in your heart that God raised Him from the dead, you will be saved."

At this point, she locked eyes with me and was listening intently. "Susan, will you trust Him?" Suddenly, her expression changed. She looked serene, even peaceful. With perfect clarity and lucidity, she smiled and said, "Yes."

She lay there for a moment, not saying anything, just smiling. I don't remember why, but I suddenly felt the urge to sing to her. I asked if it was okay for me to sing to her and she nodded. With that I began to sing "He Will Hold Me Fast." Within a few lines, Janet joined me and we filled the room with the promises of God's grace and kindness:

When I fear my faith will fail, Christ will hold
  me fast;
When the tempter would prevail, He will hold
  me fast! . . .
I could never keep my hold, He must hold
  me fast;
For my love is often cold, He must hold
  me fast.
He will hold me fast, He will hold me fast;
For my Savior loves me so, He will hold
  me fast.
I am precious in His sight, He will hold me fast;
Those He saves are His delight, He will hold
  me fast. . . .
He'll not let my soul be lost, Christ will hold
  me fast;

*Bought by Him at such a cost, He will hold
    me fast.
He will hold me fast, He will hold me fast;
For my Savior loves me so, He will hold
    me fast.*[1]

After we finished singing, I prayed with Susan, asking that
God would indeed grant her saving faith and eternal life. As
I got up to leave, Janet walked me to the door. As I turned
around to say goodbye to her, Susan was smiling from ear to
ear. Janet asked, "Susan, what are you smiling at?" With bright
eyes and a beaming smile, she replied, "I see Jesus!"

Within a matter of days, she had passed on.

The Lord only knows what was going on in Susan's heart
that day. But even looking back, Janet has said that that day
was different. Not only was it the most clearheaded Susan
had been in weeks, but it was the first and only time she had
ever confessed Christ. And it was the only time she seemed
to have peace.

It had been difficult to watch Susan suffering in her
illness, struggling as her body slowly and painfully shut
down. Yet now it was plain to see that through it, God drew
her to Himself and welcomed her into His kingdom, where
she is free from the weight of sin and sickness for all eternity.
He accomplished this in part through the loving ministry
of her mother, as well as by rallying His church to surround
her with love and care, and thus His kindness extended not
only to Susan, but to all of us who were privileged to witness
the beautiful transformation of her soul, as evidenced by the

peace and joy in her countenance when she surrendered to God's will.

And so, how do we make sense of all that happens in the world, both good and bad? We remember that "we know that God causes all things to work together for good to those who love God, to those who are called according to His purpose" (Rom. 8:28). *All* things—abuse, divorce, diseases, cancer, suffering, even death—God works them together for good. How can we trust that He will? It is because we know the character of God, that He is good, righteous, loving, and kind.

Even when we consider the trials and difficulties of life, we need to remember that a few decades on earth are but a mere drop in the ocean of eternity. And while we tend to focus on our negative circumstances, when we lift our eyes to heaven and consider God's purposes through the lens of Scripture, we quickly see the many-splendored ways that God demonstrates His kindness to us. When we ponder and meditate on His goodness to us, we are able to join the psalmist in proclaiming: "Because Your lovingkindness is better than life, my lips will praise You" (Ps. 63:3)!

ACKNOWLEDGMENTS

Every book the Lord allows me to write is a demonstration of His kindness. I am overwhelmed with the privilege and sobered by the responsibility. Thank you, Lord, for Your patience, tender mercies, love, and grace. I would be utterly lost without You.

I am also very grateful to those who have helped make this book possible. I am indebted to the amazing team at Moody Publishers, especially to my friend Drew Dyck for his friendship, encouragement, humor, and editorial skill. Many thanks to Phil Newman for his excellent work as my editor, catching my many mistakes and offering helpful suggestions that made the book better. I am also thankful to Erik Peterson and his design team for working hard on the cover presentation and for being patient with me through the process. I would also like to express my sincere thanks to Janet Shaw and Tom and Wilma Harrington for sharing their stories with me. May the Lord use their testimony to tell others of His wonderful kindness!

I dedicated this book to my mom, who suffered a life-threatening ordeal in the winter of 2022, but God pulled her through by His grace and kindness! I am also thankful to my stepdad, Mike, who never left her side, ministering to her with Christlike love. It was in the midst of this trial that I got to see God's kindness up close.

Finally, I owe a debt of gratitude to my family. My kids are fountains of abundant joy in my life. I don't know what I would do without them. Furthermore, my wife, Jessica, is the greatest earthly blessing I've ever received from the Lord and a constant reminder of God's lovingkindness to me.

NOTES

Introduction: Beholding the Kindness of God

1. Dan DeWitt, *Life in the Wild: Fighting for Faith in a Fallen World* (Epsom, Surrey: The Good Book Company, 2018), 63.

2. In my opinion, the greatest contemporary treatment of the issue of God's goodness and the problem of evil (also called *theodicy*) is Scott Christensen, *What About Evil? A Defense of God's Sovereign Glory* (Phillipsburg, NJ: P&R Publishing, 2020).

3. Stephen Charnock, *The Existence and Attributes of God*, ed. Mark Jones (Wheaton, IL: Crossway, 2022), 1197.

4. William G. T. Shedd, *Dogmatic Theology*, 3rd edition, ed. Alan W. Gomes (Phillipsburg, NJ: P&R Publishing, 2003), 304.

5. Louis Berkhof, *Systematic Theology: New Edition* (1938, repr. Grand Rapids, MI: Eerdmans, 1996), 70.

6. Wilhelmus à Brakel, *The Christian's Reasonable Service: Volume 1*, trans. Bartel Elshout, ed. Joel R. Beeke (Grand Rapids, MI: Reformation Heritage Books, 1992), 122.

7. "Athanasian Creed," Christian Classics Ethereal Library, https://www.ccel.org/creeds/athanasian.creed.html.

8. A simple yet helpful resource on the doctrine of divine simplicity is James E. Dolezal, *All That Is In God: Evangelical Theology and the Challenge of Classical Christian Theism* (Grand Rapids, MI: Reformation Heritage Books, 2017).

Chapter 1: God's Kindness in Salvation

1. R. C. Sproul, *The Holiness of God* (Carol Stream, IL: Tyndale, 1985), 25.

2. J. C. Ryle, *Holiness: Its Nature, Hindrances, Difficulties, and Roots* (1879; repr., Darlington, England: Evangelical Press, 1979), 2.

3. The term *hesed* is expressed in many ways. Joel Beeke and Paul Smalley note that "*khesed* communicates faithfulness, as in God's keeping of his covenant of grace." *Reformed Systematic Theology, Vol. I* (Wheaton, IL: Crossway, 2019), 788.

4. William D. Mounce likewise concludes that "Paul probably sees Jesus as the embodiment of God the Father's goodness and philanthropy." *Pastoral Epistles, Word Biblical Commentary* (Nashville, TN: Thomas Nelson, 2000), 447.

Chapter 2: God's Kindness in Repentance and Faith

1. Sinclair Ferguson, *The Grace of Repentance* (Wheaton, IL: Crossway, 2010), 15–16.

2. Ferguson, *The Grace of Repentance*, 18.

3. Thomas Watson, *The Doctrine of Repentance* (1668; repr., Edinburgh, Scotland: Banner of Truth Trust, 1987), 18.

4. Thomas Brooks, *Precious Remedies Against Satan's Devices* (1652; repr., Edinburgh, Scotland: Banner of Truth Trust, 1968), 56.

5. Thomas Watson, *All Things for Good* (1663; repr., Edinburgh, Scotland: Banner of Truth Trust, 2008), 14.

6. Wilhelmus à Brakel, *The Christian's Reasonable Service: Volume 1*, trans. Bartel Elshout, ed. Joel R. Beeke (Grand Rapids, MI: Reformation Heritage Books, 1992), 123.

7. John MacArthur, *The Gospel According to Jesus: What Is Authentic Faith?* (Grand Rapids, MI: Zondervan, 2008), 179.

8. Louis Berkhof, *Systematic Theology* (Grand Rapids, MI: Eerdmans, 1939), 486.

9. Richard Owen Roberts, *Repentance: The First Word of the Gospel* (Wheaton, IL: Crossway, 2002), 28.

10. Roberts, *Repentance*, 68.

11. Berkhof, *Systematic Theology*, 487.

12. Roberts, *Repentance*, 70.

Chapter 3: God's Kindness in Sanctification

1. Wayne Grudem, *Systematic Theology: An Introduction to Bible Doctrine* (Grand Rapids, MI: Zondervan, 1994), 746.

2. Jerry Bridges, *The Pursuit of Holiness* (Colorado Springs, CO: NavPress, 1978), 68.

3. J. C. Ryle, *Holiness: Its Nature, Hindrances, Difficulties, and Roots* (1879; repr., Darlington, England: Evangelical Press, 1979), 51.

Chapter 4: God's Kindness in Relationships

1. The main thesis of Gary Thomas' helpful book *Sacred Marriage* is, "What if God designed marriage to make us holy more than to make us happy?" (Grand Rapids, MI: Zondervan, 2000).

2. John Calvin, *Institutes of the Christian Religion*, trans. Robert White (1541; repr., Edinburgh, Scotland: Banner of Truth Trust, 2014), 517.

Chapter 5: God's Kindness in Blessing

1. Worship offered on "the high places" was often done for the benefit of false gods, and therefore prohibited in many places in Scripture, such as Lev. 17:3–4 and Deut. 12:13–14. However, because "there was no house built for the name of the Lord" (1 Kings 3:2), God's people were allowed to offer sacrifices on high places, provided that they followed the biblical laws regarding sacrifice set out in Leviticus.

2. "First Person to Run a Mile in Less than Four Minutes," Guinness World Records, https://www.guinnessworldrecords.com/world-records/first-person-to-run-a-mile-in-less-than-four-minutes.

3. Mythili Devarakonda, "What Is the Fastest Mile Time?," *USA Today*, February 13, 2023, https://www.usatoday.com/story/sports/2023/02/15/fastest-mile-time-record/10606213002/.

4. Jeremiah Burroughs, *The Rare Jewel of Christian Contentment* (1648; repr., Edinburgh, Scotland: Banner of Truth Trust, 1964), 19.

5. Burroughs, *The Rare Jewel of Christian Contentment*, 90.

6. Adriel Sanchez et al, "Greed, Heresy, and the Prosperity Gospel," audio, White Horse Inn, June 7, 2020, https://whitehorseinn.org/resource-library/shows/greed-heresy-the-prosperity-gospel/.

7. Costi W. Hinn, *God, Creed, and the (Prosperity) Gospel: How Truth Overwhelms a Life Built on Lies* (Grand Rapids, MI: Zondervan, 2019), 97.

8. John Piper, *Providence* (Wheaton, IL: Crossway: 2020), 30.

Chapter 6: God's Kindness in Suffering

1. Thomas Boston, *The Crook in the Lot* (1737; repr., Edinburgh, Scotland: Banner of Truth Trust, 2017), 23.

2. Saint Augustine, *Confessions*, trans. R. S. Pine-Coffin (New York: Penguin Viking, 1961), 118.

Chapter 7: God's Kindness Reflected in the Believer

1. This whole story has been extracted from the written testimony given to the author by Tom on May 22, 2023.

Chapter 8: God's Kindness to the Nations

1. John MacArthur and Richard Mayhue, eds., *Biblical Doctrine: A Systematic Summary of Bible Truth* (Wheaton, IL: Crossway, 2017), 926.

2. Wayne Grudem, *Systematic Theology: An Introduction to Biblical Doctrine* (Grand Rapids, MI: Zondervan, 1994), 1238.

3. The discussion surrounding this topic has been extensive, but two helpful resources which astutely evaluate the social justice movement are Owen Strachan, *Christianity and Wokeness: How the Social Justice Movement Is Hijacking the Gospel—and the Way to Stop It* (Washington, DC: Salem Books, 2021); and Voddie T. Baucham Jr., *Fault Lines: The Social Justice Movement and Evangelicalism's Looming Catastrophe* (Washington, DC: Salem Books, 2022).

4. Resources that evaluate Christian Nationalism are plentiful, but Tom Ascol offers a helpful evaluation in his sermon "The Perils and Promises of Christian Nationalism," Founders Ministries, January 18, 2023, https://founders.org/sermons/the-perils-and-promises-of-christian-nationalism/.

Epilogue: All Things for Good

1. Ada R. Habershon, "He Will Hold Me Fast," 1906, https://hymnary.org/text/when_i_fear_my_faith_will_fail.

ABOUT THE AUTHOR

Nate Pickowicz is the teaching pastor of Harvest Bible Church in Gilmanton Iron Works, New Hampshire. He is the author and editor of more than a dozen books, including *The American Puritans*, *How to Eat Your Bible* (Moody, 2021), *R. C. Sproul: Defender of the Reformed Faith*, and *Christ & Creed: The Early Church Creeds & Their Value for Today*. He and his wife, Jessica, have three children.

LOVING GOD MEANS LOVING HIS WORD.

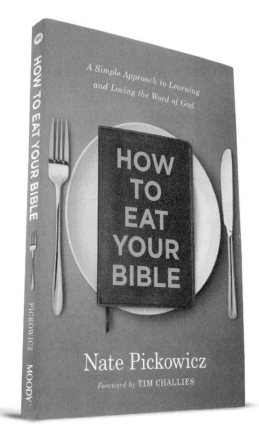

IS IT POSSIBLE TO FACE THE DARKEST DAYS OF LIFE WITH HOPE AND JOY AND PURPOSE?

GREATER LOVE HAS NO ONE THAN THIS: THAT HE LAY DOWN HIS LIFE FOR HIS FRIENDS.
—JOHN 15:13

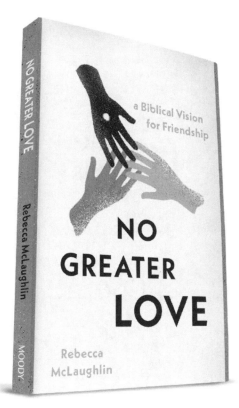